"Robert Smith's much-awaited re writing with a sort of country-soule folk-Zen heart that finds, feels, and gravitas of mortal life in and throu telling details. But his new collection is a stunning reimagining. He has written his way out from under the weight of a biography that could have easily destroyed a lesser man, and he has done so, miraculously perhaps, via the sonnet. We are blessed accordingly. His absence was unquestionably understandable; his return is unquestionably beautiful."

—Christopher Watkins, author of *Short Houses With Wide Porches* and *The Waiting Room.*

"The sonnet has never lost its popularity. Its strict disciplines have both attracted and challenged generations of poets. In this fine collection, Robert Lavett Smith demonstrates his mastery of the form. Petrarchan, Shakespearian, or the more demanding Spenserian variant, these poems are meticulous, thoughtful and accessible. The subjects are wide-ranging and include fellow poets, the weather, boozing, autism, graffiti, a Victorian razor and (delightfully) the attractions of fat ladies. Devastated by the death of his beloved wife, there is bleakness and despair, and a sense of hopelessness that reminds me of the desolate sonnets of Gerard Manley Hopkins. From such desperation come some of the finest poems in this collection."

—David Gwilym Anthony, author of *Talking To Lord Newborough* and *Passing Through The Woods.*

SMOKE
IN COLD
WEATHER

SMOKE IN COLD WEATHER

A Gathering of Sonnets

ROBERT LAVETT SMITH

Full Court Press
Englewood Cliffs, New Jersey

First Edition

Copyright © 2013 by Robert Lavett Smith

Published in the United States of America
by Full Court Press, 601 Palisade Avenue
Englewood Cliffs, NJ 07632
www.fullcourtpressnj.com

ISBN 978-1-938812-05-7
Library of Congress Control No. 2012952613

*Editing and book design by Barry Sheinkopf
for Bookshapers (www.bookshapers.com)*

Author photo by Janet Wildung

Cover art courtesy istockphoto.com

Colophon by Liz Sedlack

Oh somewhere in the distance
You and I had fought the monster to a draw,
In those days of books and wine
And Ferlinghetti grasping for a straw.

—Paul Siebel, "Then Came The Children"

ACKNOWLEDGMENTS

The author wishes to thank the following publications, both in print and online, in which some of these poems first appeared, occasionally in slightly different versions:

Accessahut (blog): "This House You Shared"

Amarillo Bay: "Medusa, Unbeheaded, Turned to Stone," "Metro Beaubourg," "The Tall Autistic Boy Spits on My Head"

Big River Poetry Review: "Berkeley in Late Autumn"

The Bitchin' Kitsch: "Adolescence," "At The Botanical Gardens," "A Sanctuary for Wounded Birds," "The Inadvertent Halo"

Brevity Poetry Review: "The Cantonese Station"

Ceremony: "The Green Rosary"

Challenger International: "Empty Classroom," "Lovely Woman, Casually Observed, ""The Marin Headlands at the Winter Solstice," "Monet's Domain at Giverny," "Nathaniel and Elizabeth, Never Born," "Nature Lives Only In The Present Tense," "On a Railroad Siding Outside Helper, Utah," "The Riddle of the Bones," "The Scars of Summer Fires," "The World Appears More Perfect"

Chantrelle's Notebook: "Dr. Hawking Eschews the Thought of Heaven"

The Deronda Review: "Ordinary Quarters," "The Reinventions of the Past"

Drown In My Own Fears: "The Netted Stars"

The Eclectic Muse: "Do-It-Yourself Crematorium," "In Memory of Suze Rotolo, 1943–2011," "My Wastrel Ways," "The Weight of Ended Things," "You Grew A Goatee"

Earthshine: "The Gaudy Revels of the Unforeseen"

Kevin Barbieux, The Homeless Guy (blog): "Like Fresnel Lenses"

Living in the Land of the Dead: "In This Deceptive Weather"

Minotaur: "Deceptive Violin," "Riots of Light Too Lovely to Contain"

Mudlark: "The End of the World," "Pleated Paper Cups," "Starr's Oriental Rugs," "Straight Razor," "That Silence Grows"

Redheaded Stepchild: "Velvet Jesus, Magic Eight Ball"

Street Spirit: "The Expurgated Version," "The Less Said," "The Night They Called to Tell Me You Were Gone"

The Road Not Taken: "A Hawk," "Force of Habit"

Thick With Conviction: "The Breathing Mask," "The Truth of Your Right Foot"

Tiger's Eye: "Taming The Common Unicorn"

Wild Violet: "Bird and Cows," "Daffodils," "Maud Gonne"

Write On (blog): "A Wind Blows Through My Days," "Gratitude," "Therapy," "Things One Has Forgotten," "What the Space Says"

On a more personal note, I would especially like to thank Barry Sheinkopf for persuading me to compile this book, and for his unflagging support and encouragement over what is now more than thirty years. Barry, you're a *mensch!* Thanks and acknowledgment are also due to David Gwilym Anthony, Barbara Belle-Diamond, Bill Bly, Dan Brady, Barbara Brewer, Buford Buntin, Susan Burke, Victor Buxbaum, Diana Caliz, Marsha Campbell, Chris Charles, Peggy Clinton, Bobby Coleman, Eric Dahm,

Owen Dunkle, Jack Foley, Hugh Gerstein, Louis Grace, Taylor Graham, Ryan Guth, Tom Hargarten, Johnny Hernandez, Sid Kemp, Ray Kerr, Eugenia Koukounas, Deena Larsen, David Lauter, Vincent Libasci, Kris Lindbeck, Jeanne Lupton, Gary Mallin, Geraldine McGrath, H. D. Moe, Valerie Nance, Wendy Overin, Kathy Reed, Janet Rhodes, Michael Rhodes, Robert-Harry Rovin, Daniel Ryan, Sally Love Saunders, C. Lavett Smith, Marjorie M. Smith, Linda Tabor-Beck, Jan Tilden, Sean Tripi, Ray Valdez, GeorgeVan Ausdall, Susan Van Ausdall, Vicki Van Ausdall, Christopher Watkins, Jennifer Whitten, Janet Wildung, John Young, and Fritz Zimmerman.

TABLE OF CONTENTS

AUTHOR'S NOTE

MORE THAN FORTY YEARS ago now, I began my life as a poet in the way so many children do, by giving in with reckless abandon to the sometimes dubious pleasures of rhyme. These are treacherous waters indeed when one is fourteen. Mercifully few of my adolescent efforts survive, and by my later teens I had caught up with the (then) twentieth century sufficiently to appreciate the advantages of a less-restrictive, and far more fashionable, free-verse style. It wasn't that I ever dismissed formalism out of hand, but simply that I realized, to my chagrin, that I wasn't sufficiently skilled as a rhymer to make an honest go of it.

Fast forward to the present day. Having published, in 2006, a free-verse collection comprised of work from the previous eleven years, I found myself at an impasse, faced with a serious writer's block that, all told, plagued me for about three years. I wrote almost daily during that time, but struggled as never before, and produced few—if any—poems that I thought worth keeping. In desperation, I turned again to rhyme, the theory being that I ought to have matured sufficiently in the decades since I last attempted it to be able to produce more sophisticated, or at least less puerile, work than I had when I was younger. (Whether I have succeeded is not for me to say.)

Here, then, is the present collection, a gathering of sonnets composed between the summer of 2010 and the fall of 2012; about 250 in all, they were culled from over 600 attempts. Of the rejected poems, the less said the better, for the most part. Some are quite simply bad; others were set aside because I feared they might cause discomfort to the people who inspired them, or because they dealt with aspects of my life experience that I simply didn't feel inclined to share with the world at large. A few, I discarded for no better reason than because I felt I had outgrown them.

This brings me to another point. In writing these poems, which span a period of several years, I have attempted to teach myself the sonneteer's craft. They succeed, I think, to varying degrees, and display my (I hope) growing proficiency with the form. All of the poems chosen for inclusion here feel "finished" to me; I have also tried to represent a range of moods and voices; all reflect who I am now to some degree, and all played an important role in the journey of self-discovery that became *Smoke In Cold Weather*.

I ought to make an observation concerning the overall organization of this collection, such as it is. In compiling the final manuscript I have resisted the urge to break it into numbered sections, as seems to be the fad nowadays in contemporary free-verse collections. These divisions—there are invariably *three* sections in any modern poetry book—have always felt somewhat arbitrary to me. I thought, too, about the great sixteenth- and seventeenth-century sonnet sequences by Shakespeare and Donne, and those by Millay in the early part of the twentieth century, in which the poems, while often numbered, are nevertheless intended (except in the case of the Sonnet Crown) to stand more or less on their own, and are not grouped into discernible subdivisions. That said, I have aspired to create a work that flows organically from beginning to end, within which the reader is invited to browse at random, and where I hope some few, at least, may find something of value.

One additional note concerning the ordering of these poems. On the whole, I have sought to create a sort of "mosaic" effect, placing next to each other poems that I know will stand in contrast to one another, so that reading the book end-to-end may be an experience proffering continual surprises. The only exceptions to this rule are the opening twenty-five poems or so, which comprise a memorial to my late wife Pat, several poems that chronicle my experiences tutoring a boy with severe autism, and a series of more recent love poems which have been grouped together because of their common theme.

Robert Lavett Smith
San Francisco
October 2012

SMOKE IN COLD WEATHER

Hands that have lain embalmed on coffin silk
Are motionless as marble, and as cold;
Their stillness is resistant to the old
Worn platitudes about a Land of Milk
And Honey. We consigned your flesh to fire,
Making an end of it. I'm quite relieved
To have no grave to visit, no less grieved
For want of a location. Why aspire
To hold some vestige of you here? You're gone,
Ash in the sunset on an anxious sea.
With nothing left to pin my hopes upon,
Smoke in cold weather has become, for me,
An acrid taste of Paradise, hard-won
From the thin winter dusk, a piety.

RIOTS OF LIGHT
TOO LOVELY TO CONTAIN

I wonder, is it snowing where you are?
Do thick, wet flakes drift dumbly through the gloom
As once your ashes did? (You have no tomb.)
Does death's relentless weather stretch that far?
At higher altitudes, snow sears a scar
On emptiness that threatens to consume
Ranges and peaks—though grief might yet find room,
Should overcast disclose one perfect star.
I've kept the snapshot taken from the plane
That scattered your remains across the Bay
One January morning ripe with rain,
The grim Pacific turbulent and gray.
(Riots of light too lovely to contain
Bloomed over Hiroshima, so they say.)

EVERY IAMBIC LINE
CONTAINS A HEARTBEAT

Every iambic line contains a heartbeat:
Lub-dub, lub-dub, lub-dub, lub-dub, lub-dub,
Blood's restless circuit shackled to five feet.
But when the rhythm stops—aye, there's the rub!
Somehow the brilliant green electric scrawl
Crossing the monitor above your head
One speechless evening dwindled to a crawl;
Five minutes since they'd checked you: You were dead.
A bitter winter—on a night with rain,
Christmas, ironically, just two days past—
The growth that had erupted in your brain
Claimed your diminished consciousness at last.
The doctors' darkest prophecies fulfilled,
Your great and gracious heart abruptly stilled.

COMA

Frozen in memory, your trackless features,
Abandoned landscape of an emptied face:
A shadowed country filled with unseen creatures,
Demons and Seraphim from some lost place.
Above your pillow scribbled screens still trace
The dreams that cross this land, though they lie deep
In murky depths your tumor will erase—
Life is a keepsake we're not meant to keep.
Why lie, insisting this is only sleep?
The tracheotomy tracks your soft breath,
Your heartbeat's neon stammer a breathless bleep.
For two long years you've lain here close to death:
Black marble statue, flesh like polished stone,
Inches from me yet distant, nearly gone.

WHAT HAPPENED NEXT

What happened next was wholly unforeseen,
Worse—in its way—than all that came before:
I would not haunt your bedside anymore,
Brain waves' brief scribbled lightning on a screen
Filling the trackless silences between
Monitor blips, like tremors in a score—
Until the night your faint breath rose no more,
Time splintered, and you slipped away unseen.
Some reckonings refuse to be delayed:
Abandoned to the stale, anemic dawn
When sodden shadows wound me like a blade
Struck on the cold stone of oblivion,
I dress in darkness, sickened and afraid,
Unable to accept that you are gone.

THE MOST UNLIKELY WEATHER

Snow is predicted here in San Francisco:
First time in years. Remember how it was,
Watching a feeble flurry coat the bus
Yard—something of a novelty, although
Those faint flakes quickly faded? Oh, I know;
I miss that bleak gray paradise because
Of how it ended: just the two of us,
Snuggled together by a foggy window,
Enraptured by the most unlikely weather,
Which soon dissolved in ordinary rain.
We only had the briefest time together
Before the tumor hemorrhaged in your brain;
I take what threadbare comfort I can gather
From incandescent moments that remain.

THE BREATHING MASK

The breathing mask slipped from your sleeping face;
Alarm bells sounded to alert the nurse.
By Monday, you'd be comatose, but worse
Was this drugged drowse beginning to erase
The wife I loved, as, from some distant place,
Speech slurred by morphine, you began to rise:
The wiring all undone, death in your eyes,
Your heartbeat's scrawl gone still without a trace.
In the blunt country of your agony,
By what strange chance did that obscene alarm
So closely mime our bedside clock at home?
The last words you would ever say to me—
"We gotta go to work!"—meant to disarm.
Then, the abysmal silences to come.

I DON'T KNOW WHERE SHE IS

"We don't know where she is, though so many tell us."
    —Emily Dickinson, in a letter concerning her mother's death

"Though many tell me, I don't know where she is."
That's my response when strangers ask for you.
It's April now; the thin sky's high and blue,
The soil fragrant. Your death's part of this.
After five years, it isn't that I miss
Your presence or the world that we once knew;
The urgency of life still pulls me through,
Each budding rose insistent as a kiss.
And yet I will not lie. I don't believe
You're in some Heaven standing by God's throne.
(Such notions make it difficult to grieve
But do not leave me feeling less alone.)
Trees are in leaf, but offer no reprieve
From hollowness embedded in the bone.

THE NIGHT THEY CALLED
TO TELL ME YOU WERE GONE

The night they called to tell me you were gone
Was more grotesque for being so ordinary.
Rain fell in sheets; a fitful doze, alone
With a bad cold, heartsick and world-weary;
Just before ten, the phone rang. In a flash
I woke from dreams of staples in your skull:
Metallic ciphers ate your shaven flesh,
Spelling grim prophecies beyond recall.
The doctor's voice seemed distant, would not say
That you had *died*, but only that you'd "coded";
I knew, of course. My vision bled to gray
Like an old photograph; weak light eroded.
My former life was done, once and for all;
A chasm yawned, and I began to fall.

ON A RAILROAD SIDING
OUTSIDE HELPER, UTAH

On a railroad siding outside Helper, Utah,
Just at first light—a dozen years ago—
I scribbled in my notebook that I saw
An ancient wooden windmill, weathered, bowed
Beneath a century of gritty wind.
The other passengers were fast asleep;
Your head lay on my shoulder; daylight thinned
By winter filled a memory meant to keep.
Beside me in the silent Amtrak car
I felt you curl more deeply into dreams:
Such moments help to pinpoint where we are,
But life is more precarious than it seems.
Years later, staples bright in your shaved skull,
I'd watch those dreams recede beyond recall.

BONE'S BEAUTY

Had life been kinder (as it never is)
I would have praised the changes in your face,
The subtleties of season. Brutal, this:
Six years are insufficient to erase
The carapace of coma still as stone,
Blind eyes turned inward toward some sordid shore
Where time itself is rudely overthrown,
The brain's black tides a glutted gush of gore.
Bone's beauty beneath gently loosening skin
Shines the more brightly, firm yet delicate;
Decaying flesh can betray a grace within,
Bounties the heart could not anticipate.
Your features falter when remembered thus—
What might have been looms larger than *what was.*

DAFFODILS

Time may absolve us of some things we've done,
If only by its vast indifference;
More problematic is the nagging sense
Of possibilities forever gone.
Bright daffodils on February's lawn
Brim with regrets, for all their innocence—
Arrangements that were never sent. Years hence,
They will loom large as living comes undone:
Soft chalices of golden winter light,
Champagne flutes where the wounded may not drink.
Try as we may, we never get loss right:
It stuns to speechlessness just when we think
The future will be bearable, if not bright.
The heart contracts; once-cherished landscapes shrink.

DRIPPING FAUCET

A faucet dripping in a peeling sink
In an apartment hollowed out by death
Sounds louder in the stillness than you'd think
Were possible. A sharp intake of breath
Seems to increase the solitude. Beneath
The mournful eye of wan electric light,
Insistent drumming offers no relief,
Instills a dull but looming sense of fright.
Your photo on the counter shows you quite
Prepared for your own funeral: black gauze veil,
Black dress, eyes that already bear the bright
Combustion of cremation. Every frail
Contorted droplet, delicate as rain,
Brims with an anguish nothing can contain.

FIVE AUTUMNS SINCE

i.m.: Patricia Lewis Smith, 1953–2005; cremated

This evening in the frayed autumnal light,
I sense the loneliness that lies ahead:
The emptiness of your side of the bed
Like wrinkled snow blown fathomless and white;
Quick, furtive movements on the edge of sight
That might be memories; some nameless dread;
Dim shadows on the ceiling overhead
As beams of passing cars dissect the night.
Five autumns since your marrow incandesced
To ashes, and was thinned to speechless air,
Since fire wove its bright plaiting through your hair,
Your nipples blazed like coals in your spent breasts,
And your beloved body—being nowhere—
Was everywhere at once, never at rest.

LIKE WINTER STONE

As death draws near—though maybe decades distant—
I find it isn't my own end I fear,
But that I am condemned to linger here,
So many gone whom I'd call back, but can't.
Misguided hopefulness cannot supplant
One vivid image that stays horribly clear:
Pat cold and motionless, a single tear
Still damp on one closed eyelid. How prescient
The steel gurney, the rubber body bag;
Prescient as well, stunned flesh like winter stone;
This grim conclusion toward which we all slog
Would be less dreadful were it more unknown.
Instead it permeates life like summer fog,
A truth forever present at the bone.

THE CUSP OF WINTER

Trees trimmed with quiet brown, not quite denuded,
Soft amber smog that mingles with thin mist:
Those who insist on autumn feel excluded,
Nostalgic for a chance already missed.
On clear nights, starless skies turn amethyst;
This is the season of our deepest grief,
Of yearnings far too numerous to list,
As lasting as these broken days are brief.
At such a time, one struggles with belief;
Hope lingers hand-in-hand with bitter loss;
The bitten moon leans low, bowed down beneath
A burdened dusk it shoulders like a cross.
The cusp of winter carried you away:
A silent death no bargain could delay.

YOUR BRIEF, BLEAK BIRTHDAY

You'd have been 53. (Not old at all.)
In Colorado, an ice-crisp winter lawn
Blushes a moment with the mountain dawn,
The air's worn thin, fresh flakes seem poised to fall.
It's not a place you loved, as I recall;
You came at Christmas, happy to move on
Once obligations, holidays were done,
Your brief, bleak birthday, daylight strained and small.
Now is "the darkest evening of the year";
Next week's the anniversary of your death.
Stark shadows, this first winter night, draw near;
Grief tangles in torn, twisted tags of breath.
The stars above the peaks burn cold and clear,
Their stubborn splendor courting disbelief.

THE DAY THE FUTURE ENDED

The day the future ended was the day
You screamed in torment on a steel gurney.
You never really did return to me—
Not recognizably—not in the way
September sunlight knew you, one might say.
The horror in your brain burst angrily
And bled profusely; there can never be
Sufficient reason. Hemorrhage swept away
The darkened plazas of your shattered mind,
Connections down and spitting sparks, no words
Left in the ruins for rescuers to find.
What great erasure everything moves towards!
The years since then have mostly been unkind:
Low, brooding skies; some filthy, soot-stained birds.

FORCE OF HABIT

Some years ago—at least fifteen, by now—
We met one rainy morning on a bus,
A chance encounter that would shape our lives.
You had a cold; I proffered Kleenex; how
Could such a trivial act have flourished thus?
You're five years dead, but part of us survives
In one unconscious habit I've acquired:
Boarding a coach or streetcar, tedious
Sleep heavy on me, headlights sharp as knives,
I scan the passengers for the desired
Face never found among them. Longing thrives
Where nothing else will grow, being poisonous.
Memory, with trembling fingers, touches one
I've never quite believed is really gone.

THE LIFT TEAM

Every three hours, as regular as clockwork,
The lift team comes to reposition you—
Left side, then right, then back again—all through
The stunned parade of seconds dawn to dark.
Two burly orderlies perform this work,
Speak softly as you sleep, as if they knew
The vacant regions you've been summoned to,
As if they too were waiting to embark.
Your burdened skin may savage into sores
Which, if infected, could befoul the blood.
Thin arms hang limp as rags, which underscores
How all their efforts come to little good.
Blind eyes—damp stones—pursue a heedless course,
Set in a face as still as ironwood.

THE FRAGMENT OF YOUR SKULL
THEY CUT AWAY

Somewhere in Marin County—to this day—
Deep-frozen still in cryogenic storage,
The fragment of your skull they cut away
To drain the ruptured tumor's spattered leakage
Awaits awakenings that will not come—
All that remains of your discarded body.
Throbbing at zero, insentient and dumb,
Devoid of any trace of irony,
Cells multiply beyond the scope of breath;
A useless artifact of life lives on,
Mocking the grim finality of death,
Though you—incontrovertibly—are gone.
Long after we consigned your flesh to flame,
A sterilized container bears your name.

THINGS ONE HAS FORGOTTEN

"All things one has forgotten scream for help in dreams."
—Elias Canetti

These nearly six years since you passed away,
My body has forgotten how it felt
To lie so close together we seemed to melt
Into each other as night bled into day.
After bereavement, words are useless: gray
And lifeless lumps of language, somehow failing
To flower into meaning, madly flailing
Against hard silence, leading thought astray.
But in my dreams I welcome your embrace
Upon the star-bedazzled quilt of night,
Forgetting morning's numbness will erase
These astral bodies spun from breathless light;
I shatter sorrow's shadowed carapace;
As pain falls free, astonishment takes flight.

EVERY BRIMMING SKY

The gravity of grief pinions me now.
I should have savored every brimming sky—
Billowing clouds so bright they wound the eye,
Each rising star affixed to dusk's dark prow.
It pains me to acknowledge that somehow
I failed to grasp how precious time was. Why
Do we feel loves most keenly when they lie
Beyond what reach the mortal will allow?
You're gone; your ashes scatter and ignite;
The sullen foxfire of the overcast
Extends no sympathy. Ordinary night,
Ordinary life: too focused on the past.
No comfort issues from this sour light;
The emptiness is limitless and vast.

OBTUNDED: PARTIAL COMA

"...you plant your flag on pain's last outpost."
—*Vassar Miller*

The dead aren't incorruptible at all,
Except as anguish. No dog has his day
Save for the one that spirits him away.
There was no Eden, but there *was* a fall.
Faced with such knowledge, dare we still recall
Soft light within new maple leaves at play,
Disgruntled skies disputing blue and gray,
Deep silences before a sudden squall?
Inside the looted mansions of your brain
Sparks flared and were extinguished violently,
Sucked from your skull, not to return again.
Your body withered and your mind grew dim;
One foot in time, one in eternity,
You hesitated on the void's bright rim.

THE NETTED STARS

"...as if in your hands you held the netted stars..."
—William Jay Smith

If in your hands you hold the netted stars
In some bright place beyond the realms of bone
Where what remains of flesh is only scars
Through which the winds of agony have blown—
If in the lap of your unquiet rest
Time touches nothing, neither birth nor death—
Are you the burning bubble best expressed
As exhalation of the glass man's breath?
Or does the glass, nostalgic for the sand
From whence it sprang, blur back into the sea?
The stunned skies incandesce: a reprimand,
An accusation through eternity.
How then shall we know grieving from desire,
And who can tell the martyr from the fire?

THE FACE ON THE REFRIGERATOR DOOR

The face on the refrigerator door
Reveals a younger woman than I knew,
A casual snapshot taken years before
Your "harmless" tumor hemorrhaged as it grew.
On the reverse, in your soft, feminine hand,
You promise you were smiling just for me,
Our love—a blessing no one could have planned—
Still in a future neither could foresee.
Should one who never met you happen on
This precious scrap of light-reactive paper,
That stranger's heart would easily be won
By such an open, such a gracious nature.
In time, the photograph may disappear,
The *image* still be resonant, still clear.

THE GAUDY REVELS OF THE UNFORESEEN

"You're given the form, but you have to write the sonnet yourself.
What you say is completely up to you."
  —Mrs. Whatsit, in Madeleine L'Engle's "A Wrinkle in Time"

Does structure order the apparently random?
A veined and fragile leaf bright with new mist
Is chained to every tedious turn and twist
Of DNA: twined ladders rise in tandem.
The credulous take platitudes we hand them
And raise cathedrals, helpless to resist
A flash of light, uplifted Eucharist,
Till dubious salvation has unmanned them.
I find I'm more intrigued by happenstance,
The gaudy revels of the unforeseen,
Where love and longing do a drunken dance
With science, faith, and everything between.
Life, at its grandest, is no backward glance;
We cannot even say where we have been.

A HAWK

A hawk kept level with the moving car
For half a mile or more. December light
Sketched each black tail feather distinct and bright,
Honed talons sharp as razors. For as far
As where the highest winter pastures are,
Dense knots of woolly bison marked her flight,
Returned to dully grazing. Taking height,
She rose abruptly—dwindled—a dark star.
Then I felt sure we're utterly alone;
Felt the cold gleam in that reptilian eye,
The vast indifference of the broken sky.
Such chance encounters freeze us to the bone—
A casual cruelty resides on high,
Takes aim from heaven, certain as a stone.

A SANCTUARY FOR WOUNDED BIRDS

Fort Collins, Colorado

An eagle with an amputated wing
Regards us keenly from a wire cage,
Her flightless dignity a terrible thing—
Pale eyes unsteady, sharp with speechless rage.
The great horned owl, now crippled, seems to manage
Despite torn talons dangling stiff and wooden;
Primps his dark feathers, plays the patient sage,
But seems distracted here, too long downtrodden.
A newly maimed snow goose, bright plumage sodden
With recent rain, has lingered rather late;
No longer can she soar but merely plod on,
Bearing the burden of her earthbound fate.
Above the pens stretch skies grown rough and wild
From which these broken angels are exiled.

LIKE FRESNEL LENSES

"The greatest human tragedy of our times: society forcing every person to justify his existence with a 'purpose.' Not all who wander are lost."
—Kevin Barbieux, "The Homeless Guy"

If not our greatest grief, it's our most subtle,
This mania to "justify" our lives:
Calm contemplation offers firm rebuttal
Of the belief that greatness always strives.
Brief, luminous bursts disclose what best survives
Like Fresnel lenses guiding ships at sea;
Once, scalloped glass honed candle flames to knives
That split the thickest fog with clarity.
What purpose *is* there, if not just to be?
A Fresnel lens asks nothing of the night,
Imparts to storms no innate tragedy,
Accepts wide waves blown shoreward, wild and white.
The heavy glass—both delicate and strong—
Insists on what was present all along.

ADOLESCENCE

"Is it rolling, Bob?"
—Bob Dylan

I could have done without my adolescence,
Though there was nothing much that might forestall it;
Some say youth earns a certain effervescence—
That's not at all the way that I recall it!
Bob Dylan's music held me in a trance
That granted me a modicum of peace;
I spent my junior year abroad in France
(Where I was known, bizarrely, as *Bobe Smeece.*)
But the frustrations later life would bring
Were present even then in embryo;
These days, I would give almost anything
Not to know most of what I've come to know.
The boy I was, the man I would become,
Were stumbling to the beat of the same drum.

SCRUB PINES ON OCEAN BEACH

If there's an art to suffering, I should know:
I stumble through my days like squalid light
Through stunted trees whence awkward gulls take flight,
Brine-crusted dwarfs that never have borne snow.
This tepid climate proffers something, though:
Sea air is sodden, lacks the northern bite;
Surf's restless churning seen from any height
Preaches endurance to the rocks below.
And when October's mildness once arrives,
Lulling our coast to warm complacency,
It's clear such optimism is a lie—
December rains draw near, and what survives
Is the scrub pine, a mute tenacity,
Crippled, but challenging a bitter sky.

BERKELEY, LATE AUTUMN

The wind bore hard down Shattuck Avenue;
Wet leaflets in the gutter flapped like birds;
And every chilled November gust that blew
Brought moisture, blurred the ink of orphaned words—
Brave manifestos, whipped to papery curds
By the relentless damp, were washed away
Along with chewing gum and old dog turds:
The sad detritus of a Saturday.
Storm clouds hung low, unshaven, stony gray
Above the bookstores, rain suspended there.
Just what the reason was, one couldn't say,
But there was something anxious in the air.
The crowded street, that swarming afternoon,
Seemed lonelier and bleaker than the moon.

A BROWN LEAF
GROUND TO POWDER UNDERFOOT

Up 101, en route to Santa Rosa,
Flares foliage undreamt of in the city—
Sycamore, maple, poisoned oak, disclose a
Riot of red too frenzied to be pretty.
No seasons grace the coast, and more's the pity;
These grim yet potent portents ruin drives
Gift nature with an equanimity,
Decree what must be lost, and what survives.
How empty, then, most things for which one strives:
A brown leaf ground to powder underfoot
Lays bare the pointlessness of all our lives,
Our petty triumphs, failures, frankly moot.
No Heaven waits in breathlessly clear skies:
Only an ache we fear to recognize.

IN THE BRUTAL COUNTRY OF THE HEART

Deep in our bones we feel a stirring start,
Unsteady weather, or a vague malaise;
Now, in the brutal country of the heart,
Something grows restless with these anxious days.
If this is love, then it's already lost,
And if it's dread, it's settled in to stay:
Each second is a tiny holocaust,
Each minute wears a bit more hope away.
Darkness detains the dwindling days again;
Fast-fading foliage—a stifled scream—
Throbs beneath skies that always threaten rain;
The tight horizon strains, a ruptured seam.
Life is a wound we cannot seem to find,
An ache to which we've long become resigned.

DRIFTWOOD

Anniversary of my arrival in the Bay Area, October 6, 1987

Against the trembling margin of the land,
Where seagulls prance and strut importantly,
I've spent almost a quarter century,
Storm clouds reflected on the wet, smooth sand.
Not that I *see* the shore, you understand;
But here, the salty presence of the sea
Insinuates itself insidiously
Into the corners of the life once planned.
Just so, the moisture bears the years away:
Before you know it, sodden weather's welcome.
Driftwood encrusted with brine's rough decay
Knows what it is to wrestle, roll, and roam;
I came a tourist one gray autumn day—
And never guessed this would become my home.

THE ASSESSMENT

Be very sure, administering the test,
Not to provide the least non-verbal cue;
Maintaining steady eye contact is best;
Speak evenly and clearly; follow through.
Turn to the picture of the Jungle scene;
Say: "Find the monkey *if* it is a boy,
Unless the rainfall this past year has been
Twelve cubic feet or less in Paraguay.
If so, point to the elephant once owned
By Scottish midgets who loved the ballet,
Unless the cheetah's grandmother was drowned
In Acapulco on Saint Swithin's day."
Subtract two points for each bewildered stare;
Add seven if the student doesn't care.

IN MEMORY OF SUZE ROTOLO, 1943-2011

Who appears arm in arm with Bob Dylan on the cover
of his second album.

I never knew you, never knew the scene:
A famous photo on a record sleeve
Shows a young girl still eager to believe,
An era not yet cynical or mean.
He wasn't handsome; if you read between
The lines, you must have sensed he wasn't kind—
"The guardians and protectors of the mind"
Could not rebuild your heart as it had been.
On Greenwich Village streets, a filthy snow
Churns into slush beneath suede-booted feet;
A tender moment many years ago
Still seems inviolate, still feels complete:
The wind that lifts your hair will swell and grow
Before the clarion sounds the last retreat.

A CHANCE ENCOUNTER ON A CITY BUS

Were she unruly or intoxicated,
You might have taken her for any student;
But she's more of a literary bent,
Carries a *book*, thinks most films over-rated.
Her charm is wholly unanticipated:
On crowded buses—in her element—
She could be swearing loudly, or intent
On adolescent mayhem. It seems fated
That you should meet her on an average day
When life's no better than it ought to be:
There's something hopeful in the gracious way
She greets the wounded world so openly.
The future's suddenly a bit less gray,
A little brighter for her gallantry.

IN MEMORY OF JACKSON C. FRANK, 1943–1999

"Maybe when I'm older, baby,
Someplace down the line,
I'll wake up older, oh, so much older,
And I'll just stop all my trying."
    —*"Blues Run The Game,"* 1965

So great a talent, such a tragic story!
Given that first guitar when, as a child,
A freakish fire left you damaged. Glory,
Surely your due, eluded you. Defiled
By foolish doctors, wrongly diagnosed,
You saw your health decline, no schizophrenic.
Folk music—*not* prescriptions—helped you most;
That voice, those lyrics, always felt authentic.
Expatriate, you wooed the London scene,
Cutting one album everyone adored;
Passed on three decades later, rarely seen,
Almost forgotten, broken, and ignored.
A stray bullet left you blinded in one eye,
Par for the course. And still you would not die.

IN MEMORY OF ED LEEDSKALNIN, 1887–1951

Edward Leedskalnin, Livonian immigrant,
Who somehow built, in Coral Gables, Florida,
The massive "Coral Castle," could supplant
The laws of gravity—the natural order—
With architectural sleights-of-hand that border
On the miraculous, the story goes.
How towering turrets rose beside deep water
With neither ropes nor pulleys, no one knows;
For more than half a century, he chose
To live a recluse, stoke a secret sorrow;
It was a woman, neighbors still suppose,
Whose absence left creation's splendor hollow.
Some glimpsed her on the parapets, in white,
A sad, pale phantom in the scented night.

THE WORLD APPEARS MORE PERFECT

A few fine flakes—falling feathery and fast—
Frost the blue spruce that throng the neighbors' yard,
Muffle car noises, lend a grayish cast
To trees and houses. Soon it's snowing hard.
It looks like something from a Christmas card:
We watch the scene through ice-encrusted windows;
White bandages brown lawns long summer-scarred;
The world appears more perfect when it snows.
Each gust seems horizontal as it blows
Across the darker branches to the ground;
It's easy, for a moment, to suppose
Gravity's been suspended, time unbound.
But this—like all perfection—will be brief:
Tomorrow we'll look back in disbelief.

LOOKING INTO GINSBERG'S "HOWL"

One sultry day in 1975
When I was seventeen, I took a bus
Into Manhattan, where the weather was
Sticky and hot. (I've never learned to drive.)
The Gotham Book Mart was a poet's Mecca,
Brimming with brilliance worth an hour's ride—
More esoteric than the usual dreck a
B. Dalton in a strip mall could provide.
The homeward trek through green suburban streets
Found me enthralled by Allen Ginsberg's "Howl";
Those drugged-out beatnik fairies on the prowl
Made me regret I hadn't known the Beats.
The "best" minds of *my* time—it seemed to me—
Were dying of boredom, mediocrity.

WHO NOW STANDS THREATENED

for T.S.E., 1888–1965

"The broken fingernails of dirty hands,"
Correlative for damage. Tom survived
The blitz, long years at Faber—even thrived
Despite a hellish marriage. Foreign lands
Don't always solace travelers, and the sands
Of time are often quicksands. He derived
Salvation from the Word yet stands deprived
Of the longevity such a gift demands.
"My people humble people?" No, not he;
"More English than the English," he became
High Anglican as he aspired to be,
And—briefly—branded culture with his name,
Who now stands threatened by obscurity,
Sneered at by lesser poets. Time, for shame!

THE PISAN LIGHT BEING HARSH

Pound read Confucius in an iron cage;
Dust settled on the food his captors brought.
The Pisan light being harsh, he looked his age,
But his brain blazed, a crucible of thought,
Unbowed before the havoc words had wrought.
"Old Ez," he dubbed himself in scribbled Cantos,
Meaning to deprecate his life; he sought
Only a fitful respite far from those
Who fancied him a traitor, sought repose
Within the tortured turnings of his mind.
It *was* a kind of madness, we suppose—
And yet how bright his visions, how refined!
The long internment that was still to come
Would strike him silent, pain his greatest poem.

THE DEATH OF WELDON KEES

These windows frame a picture-postcard scene
That tourists by the thousands flock to see:
The Golden Gate, where mists improbably
Still swirl, on days when no clouds can be seen,
About the bridge. Seawater, brownish-green
If it were visible, fades quietly
Into the realm of possibility—
This landscape hints at things it may not mean.
Now more than half a century has passed
Since Weldon Kees leapt to oblivion,
The burden of his verse too much at last;
As the indifferent century rolled on,
He stepped into a vague but luminous past,
His car abandoned, broken body gone.

e. e. cummings' chair

i.m.: warren taylor, 1903–1991

oberlin, ohio, spring of 1980.
emeritus professor warren taylor
invites a group of english majors for
tea and discussion, some walt whitman, maybe.
the old house, all antiques and pieties,
a font of graciousness, has kept in store
a brush with history quite unbargained-for,
a moment that will linger long with me.
an elegant old wicker chair invites;
i settle into its well-worn embrace.
warren remarks with evident delight
that e. e. cummings loved it. oh, my face
must have been something to behold that night:
i jumped up quickly, humbled and amazed.

THAT SILENCE GROWS

This land was pure ten thousand years ago;
The unspanned waters of the Golden Gate—
Turgid and seething—yearned and surged below
The Marin Headlands' balding granite pate;
Sun-stunted grass shone amber in the late
Eocene sunlight. Long before soft tar—
Like sluggish blood that will not circulate—
Defaced the wounded world, an angry scar,
Before the age of train or motorcar,
There was no language here, no need to name.
These hills were lit by many a dead star
Burning in silence: an unyielding flame.
Beneath our frenzied towns that silence grows,
Encroaching unobserved—still, the land *knows*.

THE CHURCH THAT SPAWNED THESE SPIRES

Saint Ignatius Catholic Church, San Francisco

Filigree steeples gnawed as whitened bone,
Embedded in a pale, sun-burnished sky,
Confront the brutal truth that we're alone.
We all participate in the great lie,
Pretending none of us are doomed to die,
Conjuring devils in the surging sea,
God in a peregrine falcon's searing cry,
And both—perhaps—in fleshless filigree.
An architecture of absurdity,
The church that spawned these spires has no name
Fit to evoke before eternity—
Gaunt, chiseled saints and martyrs bear our shame:
Their dimming images dissolve forever
Beneath a coastal climate's salty weather.

STADIUM, DECEMBER

Seen from above, the artificial grass,
Silver with frost, looks momentarily real:
Damp cold discloses what heat might conceal,
Faint changes in fake turf as seasons pass.
In rawer regions snow would soon obscure
Gridiron, garnish goal post and bleachers;
Erasure's one of nature's greatest teachers;
The most relentless weather's the most pure.
But in this coastal climate nothing stays:
Winter's illusory, Summer tentative;
Spring has no warmth, and Fall no gold to give;
No thunder moves the balding hills to praise.
Nature's half-hearted thrusts, ironically,
Grant bogus blades some authenticity.

LOOKING NORTHWARD

i.m.: Allison Lett, 1959–1992

Looking northward up Nineteenth Avenue
To where the blackened scar of Golden Gate Park
Imposes deeper darkness on the dark,
I see the mist the sunrise struggles through.
I see the bridge's soaring towers, too;
The laddered metal, shadowy and stark;
The warning beacons, each a bloodied spark.
This is the hour when I remember you.
It's twenty years since salty air gave way
And would not bear your struggling frame to flight.
From where I live now, I see every day
Where your brief life surrendered to the night,
Where the rank tide swept your crushed bones away
Just as the ragged sky grew great with light.

METRO BEAUBOURG

Paris, 1979

This guy approaches, gaunt and badly shaven,
Proffers a soiled photo urgently.
It's very late—11:57—
The empty platform echoes eerily.
No train spews from the tunnel's blackened maw;
He pleads in French that I must recognize
The strangest stretch of coast I ever saw;
"*C'est important.*" His nervous, darting eyes
Make clear this is no random inquiry.
Two great Dutch windmills, one with blades long gone,
Dwarf slender palms by some gray surging sea,
Dark pines in sepia greet a gauzy dawn—
All would grow clearer once I headed west;
Golden Gate Park, the windmills, and the rest.

PACKING A SUITCASE

Packing a suitcase well demands concision,
Be it an unobtrusive carry-on.
Astonishing, what foresight must be shown,
What we discard when faced with indecision!
Each neatly folded thing explores our vision
Of who we are—read: *what we travel on*—
What we'd still want, were pretty baubles gone;
What serves us best against life's blunt intrusion.
Toothbrush and toiletries perhaps are given,
As are clean trousers, shirts and underwear,
A cherished photograph, some cash to live on;
But choices grow more difficult from there:
Whispers of other trips yet unbegun
Stir in the folds of the expectant air.

NEXT TO A SCULPTURE
OF A PAINTED HEART

The sharpness of the weather calls to mind
Abruptly crisp September days back East,
Though this is San Francisco and late summer:
September fourth, a foggy four o'clock.
I'm leaning on a wall in Union Square
Next to a sculpture of a painted heart,
Watching bored tourists pass as dusk blows in
In tatters, and the reckonings begin.
Soon now, I'm sure, the milling throng will start
To dissipate, and night will find me where
I am, near shivering, motionless as a rock.
This town knows fog and loneliness become her;
A few of us respect her moods, at least;
And she returns the compliment in kind.

DR. HAWKING ESCHEWS
THE THOUGHT OF HEAVEN

"A belief that heaven or an afterlife awaits us is a 'fairy story'
for people afraid of death, Stephen Hawking has said."
—*From an interview in "The Guardian"*

Brilliance undimmed by long paralysis,
He lets the coldly soulless digital voice
Croak to the interviewer, has no choice
But state without emotion or hubris
Beliefs maligned as blasphemy in what is
A senseless century while faith deploys
Its arsenal of bigotry. The poise
Of galaxies sings in his mind, but this,
He is convinced, is not the voice of God.
Awareness, ultimate program, runs its course
And then is finished. For acolytes who trod
In the footsteps of prophets, death was worse,
For its sheer numbness, even than the rod
Of tyrant priests. *But darkness is the source.*

STRIDENT MARTIAL MUSIC
SWELLS THE DARK

The after-school tutor makes a home visit, 1.

To draw aside the curtains, he blows gently
On the frayed cloth, as on a birthday candle;
One day he'll be the death of me, this Jackie,
Autism's strictures more than I can handle.
The tattered twill of course remains unmoved,
And needless twilight dims the basement room;
This situation's not the least improved
By Chinese radio's relentless boom
As strident martial music swells the dark,
Until I swear my skull's about to split;
But he won't touch the fabric—*that* won't work—
Should I do so, he'll have a screaming fit.
"This is a very bad choice!" he shrieks at me;
I ditch my useless lesson plans and flee.

SKY FLAKES

The after-school tutor makes a home visit, 2.

The basement room's half-filled with dented tins;
Chinese newspapers molder in a corner;
This is a place where entropy begins
To hint at something epic. Like Jack Horner,
Lost and alone among old drugstore phials,
Bills and invoices many years unpaid,
Hat boxes stacked haphazardly in piles,
Out-of-date coupons clipped and then mislaid,
Sits an autistic boy about fifteen,
Gorging on rice his feeble grandma brings,
His eyes forever fixed on the unseen;
He has no use for life, for trifling things.
Sky Flakes, proclaims a painted can nearby,
Excellent Crackers! Light as summer sky!

THE ROASTED CHINESE CHICKEN

Languishing in a steaming bowl of broth,
The roasted Chinese chicken seems unreal—
A Gothic horror, utterly uncouth,
The stuff of nightmares, rather than a meal.
Pale, pimpled skin where gobs of fat congeal,
Faintly repugnant in its nakedness,
Shines with a slickness nothing can conceal,
As though dredged up from some profound abyss.
Yet it has aspects even worse than this;
Contorted limbs suggest enormous pain;
Perhaps what's truly disconcerting is
One detail there's no need to much explain:
The roasted Chinese chicken comes complete
With head and neck, two clenched and claw-like feet.

A DEADENING FAMILIARITY

"Sometimes maybe not so good."
  —*Jackie C., Special Education student*

In the bright chaos of his furtive eyes
Lies wariness, not curiosity:
Autism bars the doors and ossifies
The supple branch a young life ought to be.
Precise and unenticed by poetry,
His ruined rainbow is a smear of gray,
A deadening familiarity
Arcing the sallow sameness of each day.
Blunt words are torn from all he cannot say;
I probe his vacant features while he shakes
Elastic arms and roughly pulls away,
His life a dream from which he never wakes.
We read aloud together, night on night—
Pale pages turning in the failing light.

THE CANTONESE STATION

Now rapid recitations, cracked by static,
Spill into darkness from the radio:
Cadences of a language I don't know,
Rhythmic, nonsensical, and enigmatic.
Excited voices, shrilly pitched and quick,
Seem to take root in quietude and grow,
Forceful, although the volume is turned low;
Unpleasant words fall frenzied and erratic.
Can these harsh phonemes, so bereft of beauty,
Possibly be the idiom of Du Fu,
Wang Wei who honored vision like a duty,
Li Po who saw things mortals seldom do?
Such sounds can't hope to paint a wizened tree
Or a plum blossom bright with morning dew.

THE GREATEST GIFT

Matthew, autistic, hardly ever speaks
Above a whisper, one brief syllable—
It's thought he wouldn't vocalize at all
Without much coaxing, reticent for weeks.
His face impassive, no emotion peeks
Out from set features, softly passive eyes;
No hint of fear, excitement, or surprise
Shines from a brow where no reaction breaks.
At Christmas, every classroom door grows festive
With paper wreaths, bright cardboard candy canes;
Winter vacation nears, a brief reprieve;
Hesitant Matthew has something to give,
Croaks, "Merry Christmas." (How his slack mouth strains!)
This is the greatest gift I could receive.

THE INADVERTENT HALO

Old hippie, certainly—his ice-gray hair
Precariously pinned atop his skull
Though we can't see quite how it's fastened there;
His face sports a thin beard's unruly scrawl.
He's led the writing group who knows how long,
Asks only that we give encouragement;
His voice is gentle, and his spirit strong,
His presence always kind, benevolent.
One poet has described him as "a saint,"
And now he's placed himself unwittingly
Before antique stained glass, light like soft paint,
That frames his faded tresses perfectly.
He wears—although he doesn't seem to know—
A well-deserved, if inadvertent, halo.

GRATITUDE

"Gratitude is happiness doubled by wonder."
—G. K. Chesterton

A tree whose species I won't try to name
Breathes in the sunlight of a dirty street,
The topmost leaves translucent in the heat
As though it wore an aureole of flame.
In this rough neighborhood, mistrust and shame
Walk hand in hand with anguish and defeat,
With ragged spirits seeming incomplete:
Perhaps the shattered pavements are to blame.
The tree—a soft cacophony of light—
Offers a silent prayer of gratitude
For simply *being* upon this Earth, despite
Long decades spent in speechless solitude,
While passers-by endure the daily blight
And go their way, emboldened and renewed.

THE TRUTH OF YOUR RIGHT FOOT

"A name is not a leash."
 —Mary Oliver

All of our bones are pilgrims, truth be told,
Journeying far beyond their sheaths of flesh
Toward dreams of incandescence that unfold
Deep in our inmost darkness. Pliant, fresh,
They burn the slow fuse of the marrow low;
Patient as saints, they bear our loneliness;
The farthest stars are kindled by their glow;
They flare out bravely in the emptiness.
But, after all, a name is not a leash;
Naming the body does not make it ours—
It is the expectation of release
That finds us at the summit of our powers.
The truth of your right foot is that it stands
Firm and unmoved upon unstable sands.

WHAT THE SPACE SAYS

What the space says is, "I have filled your life
Without your noticing, as water does
That filters through the worn earth's sieve of strife
Like liquid silence strained through hurt and noise."
The space is all that will be, all that was;
It isn't vacant—has solidity—
It is the air where great cathedrals rose,
Pointing stunned spires at eternity.
Space was, before its opposite came to be,
Before the Mass was burdened by its mass,
Rough blocks of granite hewn from density
Lacking in permanence, and they shall pass.
What the space says is, "I am space, thy space.
Thou shalt erect no emptiness in my place."

BRUCE SPRINGSTEEN AND ME

Simply because I grew up in New Jersey,
Folks seem to think I come home every night,
Cut loose to Springsteen, knock back Miller Lite,
And sing along to "Thunder Road" off-key,
But this is far from the reality:
I'm more inclined to Bud than Miller Lite,
And I rock out to "Something In The Night,"
A tune that I *can* carry passably.
The Boss's video for "Glory Days"
Was shot at Maxwell's, Hoboken, a venue
Where I read poetry for years on Tuesdays,
And I bet Bruce was thrilled I'd played there, too.
. . .No—I don't care what anybody says—
This is one lie that might (just possibly) be true.

OVERLOOKING CHURCH SQUARE PARK

New to Hoboken, 1983,
My bedroom overlooking Church Square Park,
I feared at first for safety after dark;
The rundown neighborhood was frankly creepy.
One evening, very late, improbably,
Sleepless and grasping for some hopeful spark,
Broken by poverty and overwork,
I happened to be looking out to see
Beneath the stunted elms that rimmed the square
Elderly couples strolling hand in hand,
Thin moonlight tangled in their thinner hair
While lisping streetlights made their brave last stand—
Like crippled dancers through the starless air,
Pilgrims in an unlikely promised land.

HASIDIM IN CARGO PANTS

We've seen the Hasidim in cargo pants,
With broad hats, white shirts buttoned at the throat,
Outdated suit coats, *tzitzis*, and a note
Of noble sadness. Stunned surprise supplants
Our expectations, and we look askance
At these gaunt apparitions on the bus
Whose gentle eyes seem focused on what was,
Like outcasts fallen from high circumstance.
They're truly modern from below the waist—
Blanched denim clashing with stiff, somber black;
Their torsos are the arbiters of taste,
While laden legs find glory in its lack.
They wear the wistful look of souls displaced,
Builders before the Lord, who can't turn back.

SUN ON HALLOWEEN

I'm reconciled to sun on Halloween,
Although this gentle weather kills the mood;
Karloff, Lugosi, Chaney, chill my blood
Despite warm nights, an aging T.V. screen.
But what a tasty thrill it must have been
Decades ago, in theaters, when one could
Immerse oneself entirely in a good
Encounter with things horrid and unseen.
Thick fog at dawn, this ghoulish atmosphere
Burned off and gone by early afternoon:
No trace of wicked mischief lingers near;
No sullen light demands a brooding tune;
The evening sky's beneficent and clear,
No clouds to veil a—damn it—*kindly* moon.

HOTEL VICTORY

South Bass Island, Lake Erie

The place burned down in August 1919;
Fifty years later, when I was a child,
My summer friends and I would forage in
The blackened, ashen earth where weeds ran wild,
Hoping to find smooth lumps of heat-fused glass,
Bent coins, perhaps a scorched old kitchen knife,
Its handle gone. Warm light thumbed through tall grass
Thick with blackberries, fireflies—with life.
Decades ago, while on her honeymoon,
My great-grandmother walked the wide white porches
Just weeks before the splendor fell to ruin,
Elaborate turrets roaring into torches.
The faded sepia grandeur of that time
Survives in tintypes, traces of quicklime.

HEIRLOOM TOMATOES

Heirloom tomatoes—golden, purple, green—
Brightly festoon an ancient grocery van
Speeding down Nineteenth Avenue in the wan
Dawn light. The largest fruit I've ever seen,
They're truly frightening, and seem to mean
Something beyond the obvious. I can
Imagine such a sight might haunt a man:
Gigantic growths, concupiscent, obscene.
But these are not the red and blandly cold
Creations bio-engineered to suit us now
That leave me feeling overwhelmed and old.
Technology's malevolent somehow:
The ladders of genetics twist and fold
In combinations nature won't allow.

IS THAT SO?

"It is never too late to become what you might have been."
—*George Eliot*

Most of this week, an agony in my teeth
Has sent hot needles through my throbbing jaw
Until the world itself seemed wounded—raw—
Reminding me that all our lives are brief.
The image in my mirror's tired. Beneath
A skin grown thin as parchment lies the flaw;
Time's heartless hand stokes yearning like a claw,
Beyond all expectation of relief.
George Eliot, discarding the conventions
Of the so-masculine nineteenth century,
Remade herself, a gentlemanly invention,
To lay bare scandal and hypocrisy.
It seems to me that she forgot to mention
How aging limits what *anyone* can be.

NEVER HAVING READ PROUST

My friend Ray cites Proust as an influence,
If not in his own work, at least in mine;
Although I've never read the man, that's fine;
I'm all for narrative, and—*vive la France!*
And yet it seems a curious circumstance
That I've become enmeshed, by no design,
In work whose pleasures I can scarce define;
Perhaps I'll try Proust, when I get a chance.
In the meantime, bring on the *madeleines!*
With every bite, I pray the muse will strike.
Washed down with fresh espresso now and then
(Or with a glass of absinthe, if you like),
The taste of memory teases me again,
Its power like a wave about to break.

SPLITTING THE STUMP

The ax blade was a wedge of blackened steel
Grown slick with the elusiveness of oil;
Worn smooth by half a dozen summers' toil,
It split the rotting stump. Beneath the heel
Of a fierce season flaking wood gave way,
Scenting the humid air with sassafras.
The ruined roots in jagged fragments lay
On the brown tonsure of surrendered grass.
I was perhaps eleven at the time,
Impressed that such destruction smelled so sweet.
What carnage lay unquestioned at our feet
As ancient stars began their easy climb!
And then—as if to make the scene complete—
Your tired smile, the moon a beggar's dime.

EMPTY CLASSROOM

i.m.: Raymond Paul Noe, died 1971

The empty classroom, with its little chairs
In perfect rows diminished in the dark,
Seems cast adrift in absence. Fireflies spark
And fade abruptly in the humid air.
I'm in my early twenties, lingering where
I played so often when I was a child:
Blacktop a vacant slate, lawns long gone wild,
No vestige of my childhood left there.
These midnight windows hold a rotten moon,
Heat-shattered stars, above my adult face;
Reflections can't contain late summer's ruin.
What sad nostalgia drew me to this place?
Some splendid souls depart our earth too soon;
Yours was a great heart nothing could replace.

TERROR OVERTAKES US

"In the deep fall, terror increases."
—Robert Bly

Late spring—not yet quite summer—is a season
When leaves' damp tender green is mostly light,
Wide skies stay luminous long into night,
And any thought of darkness seems a treason.
Why should we fear this gentle, gracious breeze? On
Days like these its promise of respite
Should not be tainted by some nameless fright.
Still, terror overtakes us for no reason.
In fall, the poet wrote, that fear increases,
Yet rusted foliage wears a solemn beauty
Born of decay and all that loss releases.
We dread ripe summer's bounty as a duty;
An eager spirit ranges where it pleases.
Autumn is parsimonious with its booty.

SO SUBTLE A SEASON

Summer's a dampness soaking pliant green:
This dogged climate is no metaphor,
Nor are waves shredded on a broken shore
The harbingers of something unforeseen.
Though fog insinuates itself between
What's still to come and what has gone before—
The slow dissolve, the silence in the score—
These pen stroke trees say merely what they mean.
What has all this to do with you and me?
So subtle a season speaks to what remains
Unchanged, or deepens only gradually—
The repetition of love's calm refrain,
A wordless promise whispered endlessly
In the soft stammer of the summer rain.

IN THIS DECEPTIVE WEATHER

In this deceptive weather, time expands
Like the salt-sodden moisture in the air
That finds a foothold nearly everywhere:
Long hours fall to nothing in our hands.
Anyone who's loved you understands
Breathless exhilaration, dull despair,
A passion none would question to declare
Lasting and real, exacting no demands.
This atmosphere erases what we were,
Offers no hint of what we may become.
Your beauty is immediate—is *here*—
But makes the yearning days the more lonesome.
In the moist darkness of your eyes, are there
No promises of anywhere like home?

THE INTIMATE DINNER

"To have squeezed the universe into a ball..."
—T.S. Eliot

I wanted to avoid Grand Declarations,
For certainly the least allusion to love
Would only escalate a situation
I choked back panic trying to rise above.
(I'm awful at these things, push come to shove.)
A flicker of surprise informed your face,
Like moonlight sifting through a blackened grove;
The universe contracted; all of space
Shrank to a linen tablecloth, a vase.
You set aside your untouched herbal tea,
Called for a whiskey sour in its place,
Remarked you'd not expected this from me.
Behind us, from the kitchen, warm sweet steam
Fingered the evening's edges like a dream.

DARK LADY

Shakespeare's "dark" lady boasted raven hair,
No doubt, but milk-pale alabaster skin—
To court one of your race, I am aware,
For the Elizabethans, would have been
To court disaster. Is it so today?
Commingled in your chocolate-caramel face
Are Africa and Europe; who can say
What Native tribes have also lent you grace?
Moist velvet nights revealed within your eyes
Pay homage to a ripe new-risen moon,
Dense forests whence elaborate birds arise,
Soft summer dusks when autumn comes too soon.
Your body is a land still unexplored—
For its dark mystery, all the more adored.

FRAGILITY: A LOVE POEM

From a bouquet I sent, you simply clipped
A single rose and offered it to me
So I could share the gift. Fragility
Struggled with beauty as late summer slipped
Discreetly into autumn. My heart skipped
A beat each time you phoned. Eventually,
Twelve pale pink petals withered, then fell free
Of the dead stem, grown papery and ripped.
Once, on a plane above the jagged world,
An updraft shuddered through the frail fuselage,
And I imagined I might well be hurled
Down frozen currents to oblivion:
An instant's terror lengthened to an age,
My life a blossom vicious winds unfurled.

HOW COMMON IS SUCH LOSS

Does such deep bleakness burden every life?
The night is cold, although the weather's dry;
Late autumn overcast obscures the sky;
The sickle moon's a scimitar, ghost knife.
It's 2:00 am: you're struggling to survive
Another hour—hell, another minute—
To realign a world without *her* in it—
As shadows swarm, malicious and alive.
And yet you know how common is such loss,
How trivial, really, in the scheme of things;
(We've all been told that each must bear his cross,
Must grimly shoulder what tomorrow brings);
But her least gesture spun pure gold from dross,
And when she laughed, your limping heart had wings.

IT CAN'T HAVE BEEN THE ALCOHOL

It can't have been the alcohol (then *what?*),
But that day when we walked the Golden Gate—
My summer solstice birthday, sun up late—
Was a heady brew of longing and regret.
The headlands focused sharply, daylight wet,
Surf far below us ragged and ornate;
Sea birds tugged at green water as they ate:
And I *felt* drunk but wasn't drinking yet.
Later, at dinner, indulgences began,
And—always awkward—I became the fool.
My overtures too forward once again,
I felt your graciousness abruptly cool.
I should be over you—that was the plan—
But these desires wound me something cruel.

CONSIDERING YOU
FROM A THOUSAND MILES AWAY

A gray and hesitant December light
Repaints the plains—an image seared on tin
In some old photograph. The peaks begin
Abruptly here; there are no foothills; right
Up to the slopes, grasslands are pallid, white
With frost. Damp snows that shortly will blow in
From Kansas seem inexorable when
Such silver-nitrate clouds confront the night.
This is a love poem, though you won't believe it;
Considering you from a thousand miles away,
I better see the pieces that don't fit.
The bleak, uncertain weather of the Bay
Is its own tintype. Your face, poorly lit
By longing, seems remote—it will not stay.

PINK LIPSTICK

Exactly one month from today—the solstice—
Summer arrives, and I turn fifty-four.
The world's just not exciting anymore;
By my age, I think everybody knows this.
It's not that I've grown tired; the problem is
I've loved and lost too often to keep score,
Done all I could, and felt there must be more,
Longed, in my loneliness, for one last kiss.
This is a love poem—no need to address it—
That wants to paint the portrait of a feeling.
Pink lipstick on a paper coffee cup
Ignites such yearning I scarce dare confess it,
Stirs vivid visions on many a midnight ceiling:
Lips that caressed it, hand that let it drop.

LOVELY WOMAN, CASUALLY OBSERVED

A lovely woman, casually observed,
Has about her the aura of a painting
By an old master, shares the subtle shading
Of silver nitrate photographs preserved
(The edges of the image slightly curved)
Moments before a rainstorm tart with lightning.
These glimpses of regret are sometimes frightening;
Such beauty leaves us aching and unnerved.
A cocktail glass half empty on a bar,
Aglow with tender loneliness, still wears
The ruby print of lipstick like a scar,
Calling the heart to stray where no one dares.
At certain times—no matter who we are—
Desire overtakes us, unawares.

YOUR UNBOUND HAIR

Because I know I dare not love again,
I watch with resignation as you rove
Through stippled sun down Hayes Street, while above
Birds cry from dusty branches now and then.
Your unbound hair—a "natural"—ripples in
A teasing breeze, but doesn't really move;
Your every gesture bares a treasure trove
Of hoarded longings time will never win.
Some motion has a music all its own:
Plump shoulders sway beneath a paisley shawl;
Witness the force of folly bearing down,
Love unacknowledged, buried past recall.
I walk beside you, aching and alone;
No farther—no more deeply—can I fall.

DULL SKY, IN TATTERS

I'd treated you to dinner, bid good night,
Then put you on a bus to see you home,
Stood shivering at a shelter past midnight,
Impatient for the 28 to come.
Waiting alone, I wasn't really lonesome,
Relived each look—each gesture; *savored* you;
I felt my restless longings start to roam
Beneath rare, scattered stars still struggling to
Declare their burdened brilliance meekly through
The skyline's muddy, ever-present glow.
Some sullen clouds bent down, and no wind blew;
Dull sky, in tatters, draped dark trees below.
But radiance suffused this mundane scene:
The afterglow of all you've come to mean.

I OVERHEARD A STRANGER

I overheard a stranger in a bar—
A man of maybe forty—tell a friend
Women are just the way that women are;
It wouldn't matter, should his marriage end.
Pussy, he said, is like a city bus—
Miss one, and soon another comes along;
Saving this train wreck wasn't worth the fuss;
He guessed he wouldn't be alone for long.
His graying companion nodded in assent,
Taking a thoughtful swallow of his brew,
Answered he knew exactly what he meant:
Sex was available, that much was true.
And I imagined lonely nights ahead,
The thirty years no woman shared my bed.

WE NEED PRESENT NO PERFECT VALENTINE

There's an integrity attached to love
That lends it heft even if unrequited,
A sense of thwarted destiny long blighted
By a rejection one won't rise above.
It was this procreant ache whose anguish drove
Dante through the Inferno, whose flame ignited
The Trojan War, whose stunted glory slighted
Martyrs and saints no savior would absolve.
Shall we deny a strangely burdened truth,
Ignore the twisted yearning in our guts?
We need present no perfect valentine;
Our deepest passions are immune to proof:
Like faded garlands of forget-me-nots,
Late summer sunlight stumbling through fine wine.

IN YOUR LEAST GESTURE

Skin a dark sunset poured through caramel,
Eyes that disclose a clear but starless night—
Your presence anywhere calls forth a light
That owns the wounded world will yet be well.
Soft eyelids, gentle ciphers, seem to spell
A secret language brimming with delight,
Quiver like moths' wings on the rim of sight,
Awash with wonders words could never tell.
Our sullen city sulks beneath a moon
Weary and wan, a sibylline blind eye.
What bloodied barbs, these yearnings that festoon
The tender sweetness of my misery!
In your least gesture I foresee my ruin,
A dismally disconsolate prophecy.

SUCH BREATHLESS GRACE

Over the phone, you make a casual comment
That starts me thinking: *Life is always worth
Living.* The merest murmur of dissent
Stirs in my gut, although I won't hold forth
About my personal demons with a beauty
I still hope against hope I may impress.
Along with loveliness there comes a duty,
I think, to try and solace the distress
Such breathless grace inflicts upon the world.
The swollen sun is sharp, its fingers warm;
In the translucent leaves, new buds wait furled;
This season leaves no reason for alarm.
But, once, I tried to spell it out, and you
Seemed unaware of what I'd hoped you knew.

THE LESS SAID

"Poetry is an art of concision, lyrics of expansion."
—Stephen Sondheim

Perhaps the less said, the better, as the saw
Would have it. If we read between the lines
Of any conversation, words are mines
Studding the mire of verbiage, primed and raw.
And what is silence, if our word is law?
You study me appraisingly at times,
As if you sensed the void behind these rhymes,
The way an unvoiced hurt sticks in my craw.
Our wine casts glowing shadows on the cloth;
Language evades the burden of your beauty;
You raise forkfuls of pasta to your mouth
So gracefully I fear it may undo me.
There's no sure way to bring the evening off
Because I know for certain you see through me.

PIGEONS IN THE COURTYARD

Light claws its way through ancient chestnut trees
As you lounge idly in the palace yard.
This is the Louvre—say, sometime in the Nineties.
You're barely twenty. Still, it isn't hard
To guess the girl you must have been back then:
Beauty like yours grows luminous with age,
And yet I wish I could have known you when
You conquered Paris, turning back that page.
You're smoking with a French friend, Virginie,
Who hails from the South, near Orléans;
I wasn't there but conjure vividly
Young laughter, pigeons circling cobblestones.
The scene anticipates so many things,
My heart a soft cascade of lifting wings.

MAUD GONNE

"...I strove
To love you in the old high way of love...."
—W.B. Yeats, "Adam's Curse"

In all the photographs, her hair is dark,
Simply restrained, perhaps a trifle wild;
Her eyes—dark too—are eyes that have beguiled
A poet's heart and known it. Their cold spark
Blazes down decades, the emblazoned arc
Of meteors through Celtic nights. She smiled
But rarely for the camera, a spoiled child,
Ungracious muse behind his greatest work.
And he, the grave, bespectacled young man,
Inscribed his longing on midnight's dark page;
The penny whistle and the pipes of Pan
Sang in his verse. He managed to engage
The heartache of the hollow-hearted moon,
Mad Ireland beneficiary of his courage.

MEDUSA, UNBEHEADED, TURNED TO STONE

bust by Gianlorenzo Bernini, c. 1638–1648

The master's chisel captures transformation,
Beauty's innate capacity to appall:
Lips slightly parted in mute supplication,
Long hair become a savage, twisting scrawl.
The human grief of the emerging monster
Moves us to pity, for we see her still
Woman beneath the horror thrust upon her
That cannot be forestalled by act or will.
On the translucent marble of her breast,
So finely worked it shines like pliant skin,
Lie writhing shadows destined to suggest
Darker humiliations coiled within,
The vacant orbits of her downcast eyes
Emptied of rancor, sadness, or surprise.

BILL OF FARE

I sometimes fear I've paid for company
As some men pay for sex. Across the table,
Above your wine, I see you watching me,
Your beauty grown remote, inviolable.
At fifty-five, with no illusions left,
I know romantic love has passed me by;
My life these days feels rudderless, bereft,
A raven with a shipwreck in one eye.
As candlelight on sharpened silverware
Warns of incisions merciless and deep,
I taste the hopelessness that's always there,
A bitter salad too brown now to keep.
I'll foot the bill; we'll go our separate ways;
The meat my heart, a menu that dismays.

SOME MUSIC FOR THE SEASON

November thirtieth. On every ear—
Already—carols fall like sooty snow
Despite this tepid climate where winds blow
Coarse sea-stench shoreward, but no flakes appear.
These canned *cantiques* grow earlier each year;
But why, exactly, do they irk us so,
Rotting in our subconscious minds as though
Some grim malignancy, some nascent fear?
The cheerfully insipid, the inane,
The patently commercial, all assault us:
From coffee shops and health clubs everywhere
They stretch dark tendrils into every brain.
If we've grown jaded—bitter—who can fault us
For hearing one discordant note, despair?

WORDS FOR CHORAL MUSIC

Beginning Choir, resplendent in red robes,
Mouth the old chestnuts. Peers and faculty,
On folding chairs, applaud indulgently
While, overhead, one shaky spotlight probes
The mildewed darkness, probes the season, probes
Its deeper mystery, tries heroically
To keep God's glory shining steadily—
The certainty of Heaven falters, strobes.
Familiar carols, rummaged to their bones,
Struggle to rise above the frankly heathen;
The youngsters who produce these dulcet tones
Remain unsure of what they *do* believe in;
In their crazed world of i-Pods and cell phones
Snow's only static—not deep, crisp, or even....

KINGDOM COME

Plump *chiaroscuro* cherubs grace a dome
So high above it seems a vaulted sky:
It's 1977—late July—
I'm barely twenty, awed to be in Rome.
Muriel Lath is also far from home;
This wastrel from the Ivory Coast and I
Inspect long-crumbling pontiffs where they lie
Encased in darkened glass 'til Kingdom Come:
The flesh of God's elect does not degrade,
Having outworn all human frailty.
Lath genuflects, crosses himself, is made
Just for the nonce a font of piety—
Keeps bragging loudly about getting laid,
Some fat Sicilian whore who gave it free.

VATICAN STAMP

Muriel Lath, dark face like polished stone,
Flashes his grin in weary Roman light;
Around us, clouds of filthy doves take flight;
The sky is burnished copper, buried bone.
Lath says his mother would be thrilled to own
A picture postcard from Saint Peter's seat—
A Vatican stamp would make her life complete:
Ornate crossed keys surmounted by a crown.
He needs to ask a favor, if he may;
Might he entrust the precious card to me?
(He's off to Venice later in the day.)
He adds, without a trace of irony,
"Of course it will be stolen on the way;
People are very Christian in my country."

GRADIENTS OF LIGHT

"'Progress' ended in XX century."
—Allen Ginsberg

The twentieth century a decade gone,
It reappears as gradients of light:
Unquiet skies like throbbing scars at night,
Infernal cities, shadows sharply drawn.
Or nearer home, the sheen that lingers on
Wet pavements on a winter afternoon
When the encroaching darkness lays to ruin
Weak sunlight, as the season dwindles down.
Bird tracks on eastern snow print cryptic runes
Across the page of one more broken day;
In sullen California, weedy dunes
Inscribe their wind-blown prophecies on gray,
Famine and genocide—denied too soon—
A burdened sigh the water bears away.

MONET'S DOMAIN AT GIVERNY

Unmitigated darkness—the most true—
Descends when we discard convenient lies,
Abandon reassurances we "knew,"
And let our burdens settle in our eyes.
Strained levity can never quite disguise
The hidden harshness of a placid life,
The basic cruelty that underlies
Beauty and tenderness, the mordant strife.
Monet's domain at Giverny is rife
With struggles that calm landscape would conceal;
The deft touch of damp brush or palette knife
Vouchsafe that only suffering is real.
Scattering sunlight on the lily pond
Makes with encroaching blindness its firm bond.

A MEDIOCRE OR UNIMPORTANT POET

sonneteer, n.: 1. A writer of sonnets; 2. (derog.) A mediocre or unimportant poet.
        —*Webster's New Collegiate Dictionary, 3rd edition*

The commonest usage is most obvious;
I find that second definition worrisome.
Will these poor efforts, in years yet to come,
Render ridiculous this fool I was?
Better forgotten than remembered thus!
Better unopened Moleskines lying dumb,
The hand that penned the verses fallen numb,
Oblivion with a minimum of fuss!
"A mediocre or unimportant poet?"—
There goes enshrinement in the pantheon.
(And I suppose one may as well forget
A flower-strewn tomb the faithful dote upon.)
But—be it with derision—you can bet
They'll talk about me *plenty* when I'm gone.

A BRIEF HISTORY OF THE SONNET

"Scorn not the sonnet, Critic..."
  —*William Wordsworth*

My fleeting first flirtations with the form
Were every bit as lyric as a rock;
That this was true won't come as any shock
To readers who perhaps have wished me harm.
I've never yet encountered anyone
Who really seemed to speak iambically—
How little all those hallowed bards have done
To render banter realistically!—
So—damn the luck!—I guess it falls to me
To fashion beauty from the great morass
Of language, often failing miserably;
If you don't like it, you can kiss—alas,
It's just a playful dalliance with the sonnet;
Try not to pass too harsh a judgment on it.

THE OCCITAN SONNET

> *"The sole confirmed surviving sonnet in the Occitan language is confidently dated to 1284, and is conserved only in troubadour manuscript P."*
> —*from an article posted on Wikipedia*

Fourteen neglected lines in Occitan
Address a valiant lord of Aragon
(More an ideal than a breathing man),
Warning of struggles shortly coming on.
They plead today as distant echoes can:
The southern tongue itself is centuries gone,
Neither Italian, French, nor Catalan—
He whom it praised, crowned in oblivion.
The strident music of a feudal past
Reduced to roaring wind in broken trees,
Only indifferent weather rules at last
The bitterest reaches of the Pyrénées;
An orphaned language finds its fortunes cast
Even with things as reticent as these.

I HELD YOU IN MY ARMS, TOO LATE TO SAVE

I held you in my arms, too late to save,
My body stabbed by sobs from some spent place,
Your eyes still moist with dreams, your soft voice grave,
Thickened with sleep no weeping could erase.
Scant comfort came from those worn words you'd used
When once I pulled you closer in the night,
Tender, solicitous, a bit confused:
"Sweetie, I'm here; it's going to be alright."
And when I kissed you through fierce tears, I feared
You'd taste the desperation in that kiss,
That when the fog of somnolence had cleared
We'd both confront far darker truths than this.
My breath caught in my throat, my deepest dread
You didn't even realize you were dead.

NATHANIEL AND ELIZABETH, NEVER BORN

I picture them as if they had existed:
Nathaniel twelve, his sister two years younger,
Each with the kind eyes their late mother had,
Her African American blood stronger
Than England's pulse—or Ireland's—in my veins,
Their soft skin golden as midsummer light.
Neither was ever born; all that remains
Is speculation: music that we might
Have learned to share; some books we would have read;
An empty lap on which a daughter lays
Elaborate cornrows circling her head;
The son whose absence swells to fill my days.
They're only names we chose, denied by death,
Longings that never blossomed into breath.

THE TALL AUTISTIC BOY SPITS ON MY HEAD

The tall autistic boy spits on my head—
A gesture more confounding than disgusting,
One way he makes frustrations felt instead
Of speaking. But he has no trouble trusting
Me, if the unplumbed channels of his eyes
Are any indication, for I see
Within their voiceless depths brief tempests rise,
Never maliciously or angrily.
Moments like this, I wish I weren't *bald*,
Although the spittle's quickly wiped away
And he grins crookedly at me when called
To join his teachers. No, he cannot stay;
Though what impels him with such urgency
Remains a tantalizing mystery.

NATURE LIVES ONLY IN THE PRESENT TENSE

"The things you lean on are things that don't last."
—Al Stewart

The concrete of old sidewalks turns to green
As though the tentative, eroded sand—
Descended from an ancient, angry land—
Were not stone's feeble counterfeit. We've seen
Slow tentacles of ivy grope between
The bricks of stately churches that will stand
Beneath the sky they've failed to command
A century or two—this, we have seen.
Yet we avoid the sureness of decay,
The fiction of endurance, mere pretense:
All that we cherish will be swept away.
Our best attempts at building permanence
Linger a little while but cannot stay;
Nature lives only in the present tense.

THE SCARS OF SUMMER FIRES

The scars of summer fires along the beach
Leave blackened patches on the blowing sand—
Places the surging water cannot reach,
Where August made its hopeless final stand.
September skies are hammered fine and thin;
Graying ocean stretches to infinity;
High overhead, coarse seagulls wheel and spin
In ragged circles, calling raucously.
The crumbling seawall is deserted now;
A tang of autumn smokes the cooling air;
The evening seems dissatisfied somehow,
As though the dry dune grasses lisped despair.
While ghostly bonfires crackle, spit, and burn
In memory, the season won't return.

SEAWALL

The crumbling concrete fronting Ocean Beach
Is thick with tags both intricate and rude:
These words—could we decipher them—are lewd,
Beyond the province of accepted speech.
Yet they are almost beautiful, since each,
In vibrant loops and serifs, sets a mood
Strangely at odds with sentiments so crude;
This tendriled script is luminous in its reach.
A briny breeze gnaws through spray-painted names
Wet weather will—before too long—erase;
A gray and sullen ocean's fury shames
The doubtful immortality of this place;
Bold signatures soon fade before the claims
The spattered shit of circling gulls will trace.

STRAIGHT RAZOR

The grip, not "mother of," but truly pearl,
Houses the honed edge of a century—
A luminescence that conceals the whorl
Of fingerprints, dreams of a silvered sea.
The blunted blade is black with age, and we
Shrink from imagining its touch on flesh;
Cold steel navigates instinctively
A throat no scented lather can refresh.
Magi who kneel before an ancient *crèche*
Sport unkempt beards perfumed with frankincense;
Unearthly light enfolds them like soft mesh
(A painted miniature rich in portents)
While some Victorian cheek, pale and shaved clean
As a ripe moon, illuminates the scene.

PLEATED PAPER CUPS

i.m.: Walter E. Maple, 1899–1968; my grandfather

The pleated paper cups in Walter's office
Caught the saliva of the 1920s,
Four decades' worth of blood from gum disease,
The spittle of a hobo with a cough. His
Old furniture, since reupholstered, is
Scattered among descendants. Somehow these
Long-yellowed, brittle vessels must appease
Some need of mine to own relics like this.
Corroded dental mirrors no mouth has known
Since the Depression, gold crowns forged by hand,
A hunting knife of crevassed antler bone,
Black silver wire, a red umbrella stand—
All bear mute witness to a life long gone,
A fragile kingdom once his to command.

AT WONDER'S EDGE,
WHERE GALAXIES ARE BORN

After viewing a program about the Hubble Space Telescope

At wonder's edge, where galaxies are born,
There lies a sort of stellar nursery;
Nearby, the ailing firmament, star-shorn,
Burns, boils, twists, and buckles endlessly.
Distance assures some anonymity
To cataclysmic cosmic carryings-on;
We're ignorant of what we dare not see;
Long-lagging light discloses eons gone.
Beyond the sky's assumed oblivion,
Great nebulae—vast pillars in the void—
Spew forth dark matter like a grim contagion:
Whole zodiacs created or destroyed.
But we know only pinprick sparks that trace
Dead gods and heroes on the slate of space.

THE LAST OF MALACHI

"For behold, the day cometh, that shall burn as an oven..."
—Malachi 4:1

At fifteen, terrified I might be caught,
I read the Bible under quilts at night,
Imagining the havoc God hath wrought;
Hands trembling, cupped around an old flashlight.
My penchant for the Scriptures shamed me more
Than did the stirrings of rough teenage lust;
I had encountered moving words before,
But none that filled me with such deep distrust.
I savored most the last of Malachi,
Our sinful Earth destroyed, engulfed by fire;
A red-haired Jewish girl had caught my eye;
Between the lines I sensed repressed desire.
All this was nearly forty years ago;
The burdened darkness simmered, burning low.

MISTLETOE

High school dance, December 16, 1972

They push you onto her, though you resist,
Making a sport of adolescent lust;
You're sixteen soon, have never even kissed;
Conspiring classmates eye you with distrust
(At best) or—why not face it?—with disgust.
And she, the redhead from the second row,
Spits in your eye (she *really* does). You're just
An awkward nerd she wouldn't deign to know.
Firm, wax-white berries of fresh mistletoe
Hang pale as pustules in faux-festive light:
A shame's been planted that will only grow
As you replay the horror of this night.
Forty long years will not suffice to heal
Your burdened heart, your sense of the unreal.

THE SILVERED CRYSTAL
OF AN ANTIQUE MIRROR

We cannot live the way we once were taught,
Although we make an honest effort to;
Ordinary days grow treacherous. Who knew
Each insignificant gesture would prove fraught
With hidden dangers, and we'd soon be caught
In lies we told ourselves and others? True,
We have good reasons for the things we do;
But we have been no better than we ought
To be, and we can offer no excuse.
The silvered crystal of an antique mirror
Throws back an image we don't recognize,
A stranger's face that proves of little use;
In failing light hard features become clearer:
What are these desolate countries in our eyes?

AFTER LOSS

The edges of things in old photographs
Are ill-defined, as though weak light had blurred
The boundaries of solidity. One laughs,
But laughter through a lens remains unheard.
Grief, heightening our sense of the absurd,
Makes every image seem the more remote.
Most pictures are not worth a single word;
The deadness of them catches in the throat.
Postures, expressions: all are learned by rote,
As, after loss, we mime each day's routine,
Unpolished actors managing to emote
But not to *feel*—the worst remains unseen.
Our silver nitrate smiles will thus endure,
Poultices on a wound time cannot cure.

WHO ONCE REFINED FROM CRAVEN DAYS

Outlines were sharper once, when we were younger;
There was an edge to crisp nocturnal air;
The world—or we ourselves—burned with a hunger,
A sweetness not yet blunted by despair.
We lived each landscape and were truly *there*;
Rococo branches etched cut-crystal sky;
Sunlight spun splendor from seductive hair;
Soft moons, in duplicate, dazed every eye.
Precisely when we first began to die,
We can't recall for certain; still, we know
Roses in rusted light turn brown and dry:
The old enchantment vanished long ago.
We parrot platitudes we have by heart
Who once refined, from craven days, high art.

WHISKEY BEFORE BED

I dream of flies with eyes like vivid sparks.
Despite their fragile, iridescent wings
They're black and hairy, loathsome little things,
Leave filthy tracks on interrupted work.
Another night exposes crippled storks,
Torn feathers nearly gone. Dead reckonings
Lay bare a hopeless hole where no bird sings;
Depraved phantasms prowl the tumid dark.
Or else it seems I've somehow lost my way,
Address illegible or never known,
Wolves with lean faces tracking hapless prey
Down streets where gnawed skies conjure bloody bone.
When morning rouses me, a sickly gray,
I meet the new dawn sickened and undone.

KENNETH FEARING
ANSWERS THE COMMITTEE

"Is this, baby, what you were born to feel, and do, and be?"
— K.F., *"American Rhapsody, 4"* (1940)

Gaunt and bespectacled: a thoughtful face,
More bookish editor than radical.
Six bulbous microphones surround him, place
Him at the center of the free-for-all.
McCarthy's jowly goons are unconcerned
With freedom, civil liberties, and such;
They loom above him, rheumy-eyed and stern,
Keepers of paranoia, standing watch.
His fearless verses trumpet the alarm;
Rumors about his loyalties persist,
Have dogged him since the '20s, *Angel Arms*.
Asked if he is himself a Communist
He gives an answer they won't soon forget:
Lips curling slightly, he replies, "Not *yet*."

THIS BEING SEPTEMBER

Unseasonably hot—this being September—
The weather burns a dense fog from the Bay;
Mid-morning sun, at dawn a feeble ember,
Swells to become the topic of the day.
A sky like freshly fired porcelain
Is barely flecked with vagaries of cloud;
Yesterday's forecast, like tomorrow's, rain;
Autumn is almost here, for crying out loud!
But foliage in this climate never yellows
Or flares to crimson, as it does back East;
The dying light's just a stirring in the shallows,
A hint of distant winters long appeased.
Our sallow summer hasn't come to stay,
And, growing bored, continues on its way.

THE SHAPELESS TERROR
OF A MELTED ROSE

Two broken porcelain dishes—at first glance
Ugly and unremarkable—disclose,
To those who know their awful provenance,
The shapeless terror of a melted rose.
Though the appraiser smiling on the screen
Proclaims them worthless in the usual way,
The holocaust these common things have seen
Gifts them a value no one can assay.
Found by a soldier miles from Hiroshima,
Their charred glaze boiled up in a hellish breeze,
They were re-fired by a dawn that saw
Temperatures climb to thousands of degrees.
Delicate rims where blackened blossoms bled
Commemorate the anguish of the dead.

THE MAN WITH "YVETTE" TATTOOED ON HIS NECK

The man with "Yvette" tattooed on his neck
Could be a workman or a common thug.
How sullenly he lumbers through the wreck
Of Sunday morning, followed by a dog,
A dingy pit bull—like his master, dreaming
Of realms beyond the splintered sunlight, where
Pavements aren't scarred by spittle blackening,
No bitter taste of smoke defiles the air,
And better times must surely be to come.
What of Yvette, whose deftly scripted name
Writhes on thick sinews, delicate but dumb?
Love won or lost, it's really much the same.
Passion leaves traces in unlikely places,
Shines tenderly from the most hardened faces.

LONG SUMMER DUSKS

As we grow older, life becomes less vivid,
A growing sense of loss is typical.
How perfectly we find we still recall
Late adolescence, crazy things we did.
But then again, why try to kid the kid?
Perhaps our salad days weren't green at all.
Our breath hung in a bubble, stale and small;
Long summer dusks enclosed it like a lid.
Deep, grassy shadows rife with fireflies,
The crickets' crisp staccato offering,
Porch lights reflected in moist, upturned eyes,
Sweet, sultry nights that blossomed nigh to bursting,
A bloated moon that seemed too ripe to rise—
The future dogged us like a reckoning.

ONE EARLY EVENING IN CENTRAL PARK

Simon & Garfunkel reunion concert, September 19, 1981

At dusk, free-roving spotlights stroke the crowd,
Stoking the evening's soft intensity;
The music's sweet, but adequately loud
To reach my distant blanket near a tree.
(It's thirty years today; how can that *be?*)
Both men—still young, dressed casually in black—
Wave to the fans and gesture graciously,
Simon's Ovation settled in its rack.
No one remains then on the vacant stage,
But finely crafted songs will linger there
Like keepsakes of a lost, more hopeful age.
Guitar chords fade from quickly cooling air,
And darkness swells the calm late summer night,
Ten thousand windows budding into light.

TAMING THE COMMON UNICORN

A dream I often had when in my twenties,
Set—of all places—on the Jersey Turnpike:
The virgin (if she is) in jeans whose knees
Have long worn through. The sort of girl you'd like,
But very "Eighties," not at all medieval;
The beast, while gentle, rather ordinary:
Soot-gray, unkempt, not silvery at all,
A trifle clumsy, and a bit too hairy.
He comes to her with feigned indifference;
She watches, lights a pilfered cigarette.
Centuries ago, and maybe centuries hence,
Their soft eyes meet, a languor wan and wet.
This on a highway where discarded tires
Festoon the marsh, by the refinery fires.

A PRESSING THEOLOGICAL QUESTION

"Is God a pot head? I mean, with the hair and beard and all, he looks kinda like a hippie."
—Andres Valdivia, 9th Grade

Somehow, discussion in the Science class
Has wandered to religion, and a hand
Raised in the fourth row strives to understand
The fine points of divinity and grass.
Nor has he pulled the question from his ass;
His query, unambiguous, unplanned,
Too innocent to warrant reprimand,
Is plainly put, unanswered in the Mass.
The eve of crucifixion may have seen
Disciples sleeping in a smoky stupor;
The Lord himself—pinned drowsily between
A terrible destiny, a dreamy torpor—
Divinely sanctioning the budding green,
Since, otherwise, what is religion *for?*

THE WOMAN WITH THE VALENTINE TATTOO

The woman with the valentine tattoo
Screams shrilly at her boyfriend that he's cruel,
The bastard's only playing her for a fool,
She worshiped him; just look what *that* came to.
Her eyes are livid, her expression, too;
Little remains of her degraded beauty;
She wears her hurt as though life were a duty,
A thankless task to grimly soldier through.
Her man—unshaven, gaunt—seems broken, feet
Scuffing along a sidewalk where heat hovers.
But something in this story's incomplete:
For all the wounded pride the scene uncovers,
They sway through tepid light down Irving Street,
Their bodies touching, hand-in-hand like lovers.

I AM NOT PRONE TO OMENS

September 14th, 2011—
The day begins like any other day:
A thick fog in the Sunset—turgid, gray—
And God (supposedly) still in his Heaven.
At five a.m., the bravest souls are craven.
While daylight often bears night fears away,
This morning it seems clear they mean to stay:
Something's encroaching, terror to believe in.
I am not prone to signs or premonitions,
Being practical and of a mindful bent,
Regard the Evangelicals with derision,
See only physics in the firmament.
Yet horrible forces seem bound for collision,
Life's dignity defiled, hope somehow spent.

THE UNKNOWN BIRD

"The unknown bird sits on his usual branch."
—*Elizabeth Bishop*

On this still-darkened morning—or any other—
The unknown bird sits on his usual branch,
A dead star in his beak. Why does he bother
To greet the nascent dawn? Is it a hunch,
Some kindly portent of the coming day,
Some stuttered semaphore of setting stars
That even we, with language, cannot say
With certainty is his, or even ours?
The star he holds—to the incautious eye—
Appears a shriveled berry, darkened nut,
But is in fact seed from a galaxy
Where something blossomed forth from what was not.
The least brown sparrow need not even sing
To find eternity in a trivial thing.

ON THE APPROACH TO NEWARK

On the approach to Newark in the Eighties,
Taking the "red eye" east from San Francisco,
I used to see beneath the aircraft window
The Towers' dawn-soft, doomed immensities.
Before so great a loss, no one foresees
The roaring wick of heat, the pallid glow
Singeing a turgid river—who can know
What horrors will define our histories?
But in the decade that has passed since then,
Making the same approach through naked space,
I sense a palpable absence in the air:
Something is gone that should by rights be there.
And, stricken with the sorrow of the place,
I grieve for fallen strangers once again.

I MAY HAVE THIRTY YEARS

I may have thirty years ahead of me:
Nearly eleven thousand ragged dawns
Shedding uncertain light on dew-drenched lawns,
On early morning's mute anxiety.
The time to come eschews infinity,
Appears—from here—a landscape poorly drawn,
A wavering horizon, edges gone,
Beyond which I profess no wish to see.
How tightly circumscribed life has become!
I brew cheap coffee, and the dregs are bitter;
I live alone, accustomed to being lonesome,
Tasting death's promises in stale tap water;
Compose to emptiness my shattered psalm,
Convinced that none of this will ever matter.

THERE IS A FRIGHTENED QUALITY OF LIGHT

The alchemists, whose secrets few recall,
Suspected what crisp autumn days confirm:
Rocks, water—pliant flesh itself—are null,
The cosmos fundamentally infirm.
There is a frightened quality of light
Emily Dickinson might recognize
Unraveled on the speechless rim of night
That bares this vacancy to searching eyes.
Vast distances surround the nucleus;
Weightless electrons flare like frenzied suns;
The subatomic wasteland's tracklessness
Astonishes us even as it stuns.
We seek in order that we need not see
All things are emptiness, essentially.

STARR'S ORIENTAL RUGS

"Elle est retrouvée.
Quoi? L'éternité."
                    —*Arthur Rimbaud*

Starr's Oriental Rugs in Englewood,
New Jersey, shimmers in my memory—
A fact that borders on absurdity
Since there's no earthly reason why it should.
The moment I'd return to, if I could,
And choose to cherish through eternity
Shines all the more for being so ordinary:
A bus stop bench, rough slats of peeling wood,
A warm spring night with all the trees in leaf,
Dark windows, ornate carpets spread like wings.
I was nineteen, ignited by belief
That every fiber of awareness sings,
Sure living would be glorious and brief,
Sure, in that instant, of so many things.

THE GREEN ROSARY

What yearnings do you tally—what respite—
On the worn beads of your green rosary,
White hair a wild cacophony of light,
Thin fingers palsied by long piety?
Gaunt and unshaven, your concave cheeks show
A winter stubble of neglected gray;
A resignation few will ever know
Burns in your ice-blue eyes like Judgment Day.
Pinioned in an electric wheelchair,
You must think life a grim and cruel caprice;
The vinyl cushion sports a jagged tear,
The frame is battered, streaked with rust and grease,
And the green rosary graces one armrest—
A bauble for the lowest of the blessed.

THE MARIN HEADLANDS
AT THE WINTER SOLSTICE

The timid brushstrokes of December mist
Remake these shorn hills as a subtler scene,
Perhaps the work of some impressionist
Whose taste for shadows fuses brown and green.
Blunt cliffs, though massive, vacillate between
Solidity and vapor, and we sense,
Beyond the obvious, much still unseen—
Against such trickery, there's no defense.
It could be long ago, or ages hence,
For time itself is starting to dissolve;
The landscape dwindles, yet remains immense—
A riddle that we know we cannot solve.
On this dark evening of a darker year,
What might have seemed like sadness turns to fear.

FROZEN FROGS

Fog, at this altitude and time of year,
Resolves itself as glittering ice crystals—
Still not quite snow—until the scene recalls
A pointillism: chilling and severe.
Some local forecaster, notorious here
For malapropisms, cheerfully predicts
Nights plagued by "frozen frogs" for all of next
Week—over Christmas—before skies will clear.
Oh, Lordy! *Frozen frogs!* I'd love to see
The town of Colorado Springs laid low
By that hilarious calamity!
Only a tongue-tied weatherman, I know,
Could utter such a silly prophecy—
But just imagine if it *should* be so...!

CONSIDERING IT'S ONLY FEBRUARY

Considering it's only February,
It's striking, really, how the earth revives:
Even in deepest winter, what survives
Is more resilient than what frosts can bury.
This milder California winter's wary
Of all extremes; here, fragile foliage thrives;
Pale eucalyptus dream of greener lives,
Leaving a sweetness for the breeze to carry.
In harsher climates, deep snows maim the land;
The mercury's a fist of shrunken light;
Hard weather here makes one half-hearted stand
And then moves on, abandoning the fight.
Complacent sunlight lends these hills a hand,
Granting the elements a long respite.

A WIND BLOWS THROUGH MY DAYS

Sometimes I go about pitying myself, and all the time I am being
carried on great winds across the sky.
 —Chippewa saying

Soft sunlight sifting through venetian blinds,
Bright stripes begin their creep across the floor.
This afternoon, like every other, finds
Me at loose ends and lonely. Who keeps score
When summer's speckled days spill from the sleeve
Of a stunned season like a trickster's hand?
I do not feel inclined now to believe;
The daily dirge is more than I can stand.
Crushed underfoot on sidewalks, yellowed leaves
Belie the certainty this is July;
The sodden air unfettered foliage breathes,
The clouded cataract of fog-blind sky.
And all the while a wind blows through my days—
Urgent and yearning, wary of delays.

A STYLIZED AND A DISTANT GRIEF

"...this ebony bird beguiling my sad fancy..."
—Edgar Allan Poe

A raven, ink against a scrimshaw sky,
Inscribes on overcast trajectories
That trace the aimlessness of days like these:
Blurred commas in the corner of one eye.
Like ripping paper comes its raucous cry,
A broken sound that puts me ill at ease,
Hinting at darker possibilities
Than dully leaden waves, sea wind's shrill sigh.
Poe's Raven on the marble bust of Pallas
Decried a stylized and a distant grief;
This living bird—not prettied up at all—is
Perched on a streetlight, but his visit's brief;
And so unsettling this social call is,
The evening air goes cold with disbelief.

DIMINISHED GLORY

The leaded binding of the old *vitreaux*
In East Coast churches has begun to sag;
Buckled beneath the burdened ages, lo,
Grim saints and seraphim, exhausted, drag
Bent wings as weakened metal loosens, cracks;
Sad emissaries of a fading Word
Who bear diminished glory on their backs,
Their beauty broken, dwindling cry unheard.
A momentary flash of winter sun
In some dim rectory in Boston, say,
Revives a fragmentary Gideon—
Or righteous Lot, whose face is turned away
From this much more sedate catastrophe
That rivals any brimstone prophecy.

THE RIDDLE OF THE BONES

*"Bones found on remote Pacific island may be Amelia Earhart's
—or a turtle's."*
—Newspaper headline, December 2010

Although we can't presume to say for sure,
It seems unlikely that these sandy fragments
Are shards of history, misplaced relics, portents—
We've heard all these, and darker rumors, before.
(To navigate a world primed for war
Requires some extra-special instruments;
The bright horizon's fluid, and prevents
Accurate sightings.) On the ocean floor,
The drowned Electra, crusted thick with coral,
Dozes forgotten in the briny deep;
A great sea turtle—with whom we have no quarrel—
Basks in brown sunlight, blinks away her sleep.
Does this peculiar story have a moral?
The greatest secrets are the ones that keep.

EVEN WITH ONIONS

I'm spending ten days back on the East Coast;
So far, I haven't made it to the city.
(The heat's relented this year: more's the pity.)
New York still haunts me like a gray stone ghost.
It's hard to say just now what pains me most;
While grim magnificence is hardly pretty,
The authenticity—the "nitty-gritty"—
Is tidied up, and something precious lost.
Ten dollars to a midtown hot dog vendor
(Even with onions) seems a real crime;
This town's been bullied by the legal tender
And chastened by the heartless hand of time.
Yet welcome home the exile, the pretender—
Despite it all, our Gotham reigns sublime.

BAUDELAIRE'S CLOUDS

"Les nuages qui passent...là-bas...là-bas...les merveilleux nuages!"
—Baudelaire: *Petits poèmes en prose*, I (1869)

These soaring cumuli, ripe with soft light,
Are grander from above than from below,
The one thing Baudelaire's exile long ago
Counted a homeland, years before manned flight.
I don't suppose we'll ever get it right:
While we revere the weightless rococo
Of the old masters, we no longer know
The certainty of heavenly delight.
But from a Boeing 737
Billowing cloudscapes tease the traveler's eye,
And it seems possible to think of Heaven
As true and present—neither myth nor lie;
As vivid moments all our lives are given
Which we experience *now*, before we die.

THE LEMON-YELLOW PICKUP TRUCK

The lemon-yellow pickup up the street
Is quite a fixture in our neighborhood.
The rounded fenders and the bulbous hood,
Wide whitewall tires, the chrome gone soft with heat,
Flatbed with varnished wooden railings (sweet!),
Place it in the late forties, though it could
Perhaps be somewhat earlier. It's stood
In the same parking spot for weeks, to greet
My tired steps each evening as I come
Emptied and stumbling from the bus stop, done
With one more pointless day and headed home.
I cannot drive a truck—I don't own one—
And yet, for just a moment, I'm less lonesome,
Cheered by this vestige of an age long gone.

FOUR-LEAF CLOVER

March and St. Patrick's Day set me to thinking
How humble shamrocks charm the Irish rover.
(Myself, I think I'm luckiest when *drinking*,
Cherish those nights from which I must recover.)
Perhaps I've overlooked a four-leaf clover
Among the unkempt grass of the Panhandle
Where sun-drenched eucalyptus shadows hover,
Damp earth and dog piss scent the air like scandal—
Whatever luck I'm due can't hold a candle
To sights and smells like these, not even spring,
And yet the weather has things well in hand. I'll
Scarce trade so fine a day for anything.
That precious four-leaf clover still eludes me;
I'm managing without it splendidly.

THE HIDEOUS

The hideous can be surprisingly,
Abruptly grand, in the right circumstance—
Consider, for example, a glass fly
Blown long ago in nineteenth-century France:
Huge compound eyes, minutely rendered hair,
Speak truly to a master craftsman's art;
Admiring it, we're nonetheless aware
The horror of it nearly stops the heart.
Likewise the downy-feathered pterodactyl
Suspended in the great exhibit hall,
A winged, ungainly lizard that, in fact, still
Generates nightmares to dismay us all.
How patiently skilled artisans created
Images none would dare see animated!

THE REINVENTIONS OF THE PAST

For a friend who fears he is a failure.

Our bodies thicken as our hair grows thin.
The lines of others' faces seem to blur
Into our memories of who they were;
The reinventions of the past begin.
Daylight arrives, weakened like watered gin,
A pallid glow familiar at this season,
With many damning proofs of daily treason;
Skies are as scorched and brittle as stretched skin.
Argue in vain that we did all we could;
That there was never really any choice—
Our noblest efforts came to nothing good.
Despite all this, the March rain is a voice
Still whispered on the roofs of childhood,
A reassurance, sounding grace and poise.

ON THE ESPLANADE

Richmond District, San Francisco

Washington High School—1936—
A gray art deco phantom on a hill,
A campus where the air is never still,
Weak daylight's always up to its old tricks.
What alchemist would dare conspire to fix
The afternoon in amber, work his will
On one damp moment and preserve its chill,
Affix eternity to these old bricks?
The students lingering on the Esplanade,
Whose blue tattoos bloom through their pimpled skin,
May meet your gaze a moment, risk a nod,
But neither they, nor time, will let you in.
Their faces, guarded as the grim façade,
Betray no exaltation, no chagrin.

THE PENISES

The penises—carved wood or molded plastic—
Rise in a row atop a cardboard table,
Erect to a degree that seems fantastic:
The stuff of myth, erotic epic, fable.
Since this is our high school's spring festival
These artifacts demand a double-take;
At first I scarce believe my eyes at all,
Suspect a prank, some sort of lewd mistake.
In fact, the school nurse arranged them there,
And these dismembered dicks are *mannequins*.
Soon all the best-dressed genitals will wear
Condoms to clothe a multitude of sins.
(And the *next* booth, if I am not mistaken,
Sells fresh-dipped strips of chocolate-covered bacon!)

THE BLEAK PARADE

The charnel house of teenage fashion grows
More gruesome and unsettling every day:
From tee shirts to expensive business clothes,
The iconography of plague holds sway.
A fine silk blouse, in silkscreen, may display
Grim heaps of shattered skulls and moldered bones;
Expenses these kids struggle to defray
Keep them supplied with griefs each fully owns.
Nothing about this bleak parade atones
For seeing a brother or best friend gunned down
And left for lost—spilled blood and stifled groans—
By strangers from another part of town.
Death's so familiar it's become a style;
Their lives are brutal, pointless, brief, and vile.

FOR A FORMER STUDENT, SHOT TO DEATH

i.m.: Frederick Maye, 1987–2011

I haven't learned the details of your death
Except to gather several shots were fired.
Blood-soaked beneath a freeway, you expired,
Your young life pointless, terrifying, and brief.
The body count invites frank disbelief
When I consider all the kids I've known
Who've overdosed, been ruthlessly gunned down
Or carted off to prison, some for life.
About you, I remember very little:
Our meetings were infrequent, sadly few;
Perhaps you had already joined the battle
That one day would destroy you—but who knew?
Good-looking, light-complected, always cheerful,
Prone to the horseplay adolescents do.

HÔTEL DES INVALIDES

Paris, Spring 1979

The former hospice housed Napoleon's tomb
Beneath the gilded splendor of a dome;
Tucked in a more obscure wing was a room
Where amputees and handicapped were welcome
To test their skill at fencing—although some
Wielded swords from anchored wheelchairs
Locked in position so crossed blades struck home
Within a hair's breadth of their mustache hairs.
(Thank god the mesh mask every duelist wears
Discouraged accidental injury!)
A chance to face their pinioned overtures
Such seated sparring once afforded me—
But I could *walk*, and would not be laid low,
Too proud to challenge any legless foe.

A TODDLER'S BUBBLE WAND

It's New Year's morning, twenty-odd years ago;
I'm hanging with old friends on the East Coast,
Still blurry-eyed from last night's midnight toast,
The mercury at four degrees below.
Now, for some reason we may never know,
Our hostess has a toddler's bubble wand
Of which she seems inordinately fond;
We step into the drifting yard and blow.
Bright, perfect spheres rise through the timid light
That blunts the sky near every major city.
Although it's still the middle of the night,
We see them clearly, delicate and pretty.
They freeze in seconds, shattered in mid-flight;
Sharp fragments mar fresh snow, beyond our pity.

IMAGINARY FRIEND

Imaginary friend—let's call him Boz—
Seems just as real and solid as can be.
His is a visage every reader knows:
The graying, unruly hair, the thin goatee.
He shares the secrets of his art with me,
And I in turn escort him through a time
Undreamt of in the nineteenth century—
Stuttering light displacing brick and grime.
Down neon streets melodic hours still chime,
Though this is San Francisco, never London;
However suave the modern face of crime,
Tricksters endure, time-honored scams go on.
In pubs and bars, familiar toasts are raised;
He drinks it in, bemused and yet amazed.

RUSTIC LEGEND

"The lemmings used for White Wilderness...*did not jump off the cliff, but were in fact launched off the cliff using a turntable."*
—*from an article posted on Wikipedia*

Allegedly faked in 1955
By Disney pictures—a deliberate hoax—
This stands among the more elaborate jokes
Film has bequeathed us. Nothing could survive
That headlong plunge to icy seas alive.
A hidden turntable hurled them from a cliff,
Dispatching thousands of the beasts forthwith:
On such gratuitous cruelties we thrive.
That is, if we believe the rustic legend.
Dramatic footage mounted to deceive
A gullible public, scam the scientists,
Derail the great migrations—to what end?
Don't we know better than to disbelieve
In nature's dark and unexpected twists?

HELIUM BALLOON

Through the side window of the Sacred Grounds,
Beyond the neon teaser *nO s'eeffoC,*
A helium balloon drifts down the block
Along the stippled street where light abounds.
It bumps against a lamp post, then rebounds,
Borne upward on warm currents, shimmering
Against ripe foliage like a nascent wing
One afternoon whose mildness quite astounds.
What careless hand unloosed a silver bauble
To seek its fortune in a cloudless sky,
A mirrored simulation of a bubble
That seems as much to stumble as to fly?
Although it may gain nothing for its trouble
Perhaps it will grow graceful by and by.

BUOY DRIFTING OFF THE GOLDEN GATE

Steel cylinder offshore framed by your window,
It bobs in gray salt water like a cork
While tentative spring sunlight does its work,
Inscribing fire on waves thrust to and fro.
Just so, a century or more ago,
A wooden marker pierced encroaching dark
Whose pitch-soaked wick gave forth a timid spark,
Stars sharp above and unplumbed depths below.
In the calm afternoon the buoy seems
Some painter's nautical embellishment
Thus tethered to the turning tide that teems
With kelp, debris of dubious intent.
And what is worthless, what the stuff of dreams?
What passage will ill winds aid or prevent?

THE ABYSS

This afternoon I stared down the abyss,
Just for an instant, but it was enough:
I glimpsed the void that has us by the scruff
Of all our necks. There is no cure for this
Hard reckoning, this cold unflinching kiss,
This inner vertigo that seems to snuff
Out everything at once. The light's worn rough,
The sky uncertain. Life is what it is.
I have become accustomed to despair,
But not to hopeless weeks deprived of sleep:
Sharp shards of sun impaled in your hair
Are not mementos one would choose to keep—
Distracted eyes, nor perfume that you wear—
Not when such tortured longings run so deep.

LADDERS OF SHADOW

The northern tower of the Golden Gate
Prints a deformed penumbra on the Headlands:
The hour's still early, but the season late;
Such *clarity* this cooling air demands!
Wrinkled against bare cliffs, ladders of shadow—
Visually crisp—emerge as metaphor:
I might have found them striking long ago;
Now, twisted rungs of darkness underscore
My giddy climb through past, toward coming, years:
Late-blooming love abruptly torn away;
Erasure that inexorably nears;
Ash of this flesh dispersed and gone someday;
Wind-scattered cinders joining my late wife—
The ladders' end is hidden from this life.

A SUITABLE VEIN

Beneath the pale, pierced skin of my forearm
The grim phlebotomist again pokes through
A suitable vein, and grows afraid to harm
Thin, hair-like vessels where spilled blood pools blue.
I'm stranded in the chair—not much to do—
Hell-bent on typing with my one free hand,
Keyboard and monitor on a rack (who *knew?*)
That sways unsteadily at my least command.
My blood becomes a precious contraband;
When they specifically harvest only platelets,
Discarded plasma is recycled, and
(Insert your choice of juicy epithets)
Reintroduced to the bewildered stream,
As strange, almost untoward, as that may seem.

THE STRENGTH

When I was seventeen, I pressed a blade
Against the bald translucence of my wrist;
I heard the deadened drum my heartbeat made;
I felt the void I struggled to resist.
These days I'm not quite such an optimist:
I know the edge, a hair-like thread of cold,
But I know too the strength in a clenched fist;
And I'm resigned that my resolve must hold.
When young, we brood on death; as we grow old,
We trust the limping light on Winter's lawn
Is miracle enough to make us bold—
The frozen skies care nothing once we're gone,
Oblivion's release not lightly earned;
This much (at least) I'm fairly sure I've learned.

LOVE AND THE WEATHER

Love and the weather have nothing to do
With one another really, in much the way
That old song we depend on to pull through—
Penned by a stranger—doesn't really say
What chance has brought to it. The heart *won't* break,
Though one can tear a paper valentine;
Deep grief should not be pinned to one mistake;
There is no happy ending, grand design.
Fog pools like loss around the Golden Gate,
But this is just an accident of air;
The turgid tides, worn rough as gray-green slate,
Churn with no hidden help: Such things don't care.
Love and the weather stumble as they must
Through days when all we cherish falls to rust.

ICED COFFEE

Iced coffee sipped in Internet cafés
Can't numb the tedium of afternoons.
When life has lost all power to amaze,
Regrets are measured with cheap plastic spoons.
Shrink-wrapped beneath the cellophane of days—
Bar-coded by wan light that slants through blinds—
We've passed whole decades in a caffeine daze
While disappointment endlessly rewinds.
For less than this, strong men have lost their minds;
For less than this, the beautiful grow frail;
Each blended mocha, cappuccino, finds
Once-perfect skin gone freckled, cracked, and pale.
Outside, stars sharpen. Bloated and alone,
The plump, half-eaten moon's a lemon scone.

THERAPY

The doctor, tweedy with indifference,
Maintains a sort of amicable distance,
May or may not be listening, and I sense
That little more than random happenstance
Guides any counsel he may give. Perchance
He's disconnected from the present tense?
Or is it my reluctance that prevents
Substantial progress? Silence seems immense.
Then all at once this supercilious shrink
Jerks forward in his leather chair and says,
"What are you, *crazy?*" Speechless—stunned—I blink
In frank astonishment. Not hard to guess
He's flustered, stammering, "I mean...I think
That might prove harmful to the healing process."

CIGAR STORE INDIAN

I gape in frank amazement as I pass:
Such peerless calm depicted on this face!
A nineteenth-century icon of a race
Esteemed as noble yet dismissed as crass.
These days I'd guess it must be fiberglass;
A gaping hole proclaims a hollow base;
The honey-brown complexion's a disgrace,
Acrylic feigning spruce or sassafras.
And it's a true anachronism here
Among the Jaguars and the SUVs,
The conscience of some disregarded year,
Whose damning judgments nothing can appease;
Whose grimly molded gaze, wise yet severe,
Outlasts our shallow era by degrees.

CROSS BUCKS

At railroad crossings all across the West
Gaunt cross bucks stand in silent crucifixion
Like ghosts who, having given life their best,
Are shouldering some hideous affliction.
As a young child, I was much impressed
With windmills, water towers, and the like—
Structures whose holiness defied description,
Where lightning always seemed about to strike.
The rotted tie, the rusted wrought iron spike,
Endure the cross bucks' red, unflinching gaze;
Beyond their rigid postures of dislike
Bright rails stretch out unto the End of Days.
In Heaven, only cross bucks will remain;
The high, thin whistle of a lonesome train.

A WINSLOW HOMER KIND OF LIGHT

"It looked as if a night of dark intent
Was coming..."
          —Robert Frost

Beyond the surf line, out in deeper water,
The ocean unexpectedly grows bright:
Wind-shriven waves like axes honed for slaughter,
The light a Winslow Homer kind of light.
This ragged coast seems ready to ignite;
Breakers that spew and foam, their rage unspent,
Start me to thinking Robert Frost was right;
We're headed for a night of dark intent.
Painting and poetry cannot prevent
The daily pain that permeates our lives,
The anxious undertow of discontent;
Art fashions triumph out of what survives.
A raft of churning radiance drifts offshore;
Its splendor startles; it need do no more.

DEAD RECKONING

These days we pilot by dead reckoning
Without the aid of steady star or chart:
Familiar constellations fly apart,
And we're no longer sure of anything.
The GPS—dispassionate, unerring—
Should reassure us, but the journey's heart
Eludes us, although all our phones are smart;
We distrust such precise positioning.
No constant seaman's clock calls us to courage
Where time itself asserts no sovereignty:
Like superstitious sailors clutching wreckage,
We skirt the rim of chaos gingerly,
Bewildered navigators of the age
Who've never really even put to sea.

CHRISTIAN RUBBER DUCKY

What possible excuse for this anomaly
Is there? It seems to trivialize the Lord;
Most humanists, who've openly abhorred
Religion, still find it tasteless. What a homily
One could construct around it! *Homily?*
Righteous disgust might strike the proper chord;
The outraged faithful surely can afford
A modicum of anger. At least nominally,
It seems innocuous, a children's toy,
A tiny silver cross around its neck,
Avian face cartoonish, cloyingly cute.
What but design of darkness to annoy
Induced the toy makers to go this route,
Reducing holiness to outright *dreck?*

VERBATIM—OR NEAR ENOUGH

I got me an appointment with a demon
Tomorrow night at midnight in the bone yard,
The darkest corner—where the ground is hard—
An hour when can't nobody hear you screamin'.
I know I ain't going there to meet no woman:
This here's one club where women have been barred.
Could be my life has always been ill-starred;
Now, sure as shit, there's something awful comin'.
I knew when I first saw that evil eye
On some old lady over there on Haight,
A kind of agitation in the sky,
The way thick shadows seemed to take on weight.
Won't be too long now 'fore I'm bound to die;
You can't put off such things—they just won't wait.

THE GREAT CAFFEINE COMMUNION

The coffee at First Cup is rich and hot,
Ripens the aromatic morning dark;
Four silver cylinders—each one a pot—
Shine in the shadows, quietly at work.
The middle-aged baker—Asian, amiable—
Balances trays of freshly baked croissants:
His lighted counter and glass shelves are full
Of doughnuts, cookies, all our mortal wants.
But neither taste nor smell compels us here:
Angelic choirs pour from his radio,
Gently admonish that the Lord is near,
Salvation sweet as newly risen dough.
Somnambulant commuters struggle in,
Heads bowed before the great caffeine communion.

YOU LOSE YOUR PARENTS BIT BY BIT

It's said you lose your parents bit by bit
As they grow older, and I've found it's true.
A table saw (while scarcely requisite)
May help to separate a joint or two.
My father—a reluctant 84—
Playing with his power tools on Christmas Eve,
Ran afoul of said unforgiving saw,
Blood everywhere like you would not believe!
Now, Dad's a scientist down to the marrow,
And seemed if anything somewhat intrigued;
His right-hand pinky's gone, but by tomorrow
He'll be just fine: at worst, a bit fatigued.
Dad loves an unfamiliar situation,
And this was not a drastic amputation.

EVEN A MAIMED HAND
EASILY HOLDS A BRUSH

Recovering from his recent amputation,
My dad enjoys the watercolorist
On PBS—a dubious compensation,
Since he still likes woodworking programs best.
Elaborate doodads turned out on a lathe,
Delicate brush strokes, vie for his attention,
The pinky that the surgeon couldn't save
A badge of honor he takes pains to mention.
Even a maimed hand easily holds a brush,
And Dad's considering an artist's life
Despite the implements applying the wash
Being no more caustic than a palette knife.
He'd learn to paint, but what sticks in his craw
Is that the craft demands no table saw.

FOG ON THE MEADOW, GOLDEN GATE PARK

Just before dawn—the sky already gray—
Fog pools above a meadow in the park:
Ephemeral echo of the coming day,
Bright ornament of the departing dark.
The climate, and the season, do their work;
One might imagine that the mist is snow
Clinging to peeling eucalyptus bark,
This transitory winter all we know.
Frost blanched such mornings centuries ago
Before the frenzied, apoplectic sky
Throbbed with a sickly, never-ending glow,
Duping the darkness with a luminous lie.
Damp daylight drains away a pale illusion,
As though the sun resented time's intrusion.

THE PILGRIMS' TURKEY

The Pilgrims' turkey was a scrawny creature
Still capable of flight but, nonetheless,
In that grim wilderness, a welcome feature
At their near-barren table. Who could bless
So frightening a world? Strained thankfulness—
Despite the threats of famine and disease,
The grave and silent natives, and the less
Than gracious forest's darkly marshaled trees
Whose furtive rustlings brought them to their knees,
Timid and trembling—moved them still to praise.
Abashed before the Lord they sought to please,
Broken hosannas rimmed their numbered days.
The bird's flesh bore the taste of isolation,
Wood smoke and terror, pious resignation.

CROSSES DRAPED WITH FLOWERS

Along the desolate highways of the West
One sometimes sees plain crosses like sucked bones,
Their pallor bloodied by dawn's slaughter, stones
From the surrounding desert rudely pressed
Against their bases. Here too are garlands dressed
By the brute patience of decay, dull groans
Of restless weather through a land that owns
Death and dismay, forsaking all the rest.
These are not graves but monuments to those
Who perished in collisions near the place
And now are souls arrayed in speechless fire.
Dry heat has scorched the petals of the rose,
The wilting lily, hyacinth's blue spire—
All brown and crisp as old Castilian lace.

MILITARY CEMETERY, THE PRESIDIO

The light's so strident, marble markers seem
To blaze against the darkness of the grass:
Row after row of polished headstones gleam
Like perfect teeth through which groundskeepers pass
On roaring mowers, unmindful of the dead
Who doze beneath the rotor's shining wake.
(Thus crocodile teeth are cleaned—it's said—
By gentle birds whom savage jaws could break.)
A name, a rank, a graven date of death,
Perhaps a passing mention of a war,
A stillness like a held-forever breath:
These sacrifices come to little more.
And on the cold reverse of many a stone
A widow's name, she too now decades gone.

LAUDANUM

Tincture of alcohol and opium,
You lit the nineteenth century's greatest minds!
Bedeviled by gout, Collins drew the blinds,
Swallowed the draught, and felt the world go numb.
His great friend Dickens mingled with the scum
Of London in the riverside drug dens,
And, having seen his visions, he went thence,
Left *Drood* to generations yet to come.
The oil lamp and the tallow candle burn
With an unearthly radiance, beckoning
To dark, demonic shades at every turn;
The blood's polluted with an evil thing,
Ash going cold within a funeral urn;
Each tortured moment is a reckoning.

BAUDELAIRE BEFORE THE MIRROR

"When he looked into the mirror, he often greeted his own image,
not recognizing whose it was."
    —André Breton, on Baudelaire

In many photographs he looks like me,
Save that he's stubbled, and I wear a beard.
The thinning hair, the sunken eyes that see
Life's mordant ugliness: The parallel's weird.
And when I read of his mulatto mistress,
I had to wonder about previous lives.
Perhaps the thing that most unites us is
We both stared down the void just to survive.
And what if Baudelaire, before the mirror,
Had seen the wasted shade I am today?
Would we regard each other without fear?
What words would be exchanged, what *could* we say?
I think moonlight's decay would dare reveal,
Adrift in darkened silver, the unreal.

THE WAY THE WORLD ONCE FELT
BUT WON'T AGAIN

The way the world once felt but won't again—
Frost-sharp Orion leaning in the east,
Winds off the Hudson shoveling the creased
Snow up against the fence posts—winter, then,
Was still a magic season, evenings when
My misted breath was mingled with my dog's
On long walks after dinner, when Yule logs
Blazed on the T.V. screen. What was I—ten,
Perhaps a few years older? I can count
On one hand the rare moments in my life
When I had faith I really would amount
To something, when the chilled air was a knife
Whose blade struck forth bright sparks of hope. I don't
Expect much these days; mostly I survive.

THE END OF DAYS

These are the years a writer friend once called
"The science fiction years." We have arrived
At the millennium and yet survived
Past all predictions, doom again forestalled.
Apocalypse seems far away today,
Cloudless November suddenly grown warm;
How can such fine surroundings come to harm
While sunlit waves trace scriptures on the Bay?
As twilight falls, what the mild darkness says
Seems cause enough to look ahead with hope;
Bright breathing foliage, free from all malaise,
Foretells a future limitless in scope.
Those fools who now proclaim the End of Days
Will hang themselves if given enough rope.

THE END OF THE WORLD

A truck arrayed with angels, gaudy stars,
Struggles through traffic in the Civic Center,
Emblazoned with grim quotes from scripture verse
Admonishing the End is surely near.
("The Bible guarantees it!") Weather's clear,
The morning warm, fragrant with budding spring.
How can the heart be yoked to senseless fear
On such a glorious day? No reckoning
Seems in the offing while such songbirds sing
So sweetly to the old procreant urge;
The spreading sky presents a dazzling
Blue slate on which creation is writ large.
Will Armageddon show May twenty-first?
We've got another year or two, at worst!

IT'S NEVER BEEN A POSE

"You do sad so good."
    —Barry Sheinkopf

It's never been a literary pose:
Deep sadness festers when I feel alone,
A hopelessness I ought to have outgrown,
Worse than it is for most folks, I suppose.
I dread the thorn but seldom see the rose;
This life—sucked dry, sharp-splintered as a bone—
In which I so reluctantly am thrown,
Emphatically is *not* a path I chose.
Concerning love, I've stumbled utterly
Oftener than not; I've made the fatal error
Of truly treating women decently,
Met with disdain that only fueled my terror.
Of course, these words can't claim to solace me;
Our heartless world, for this, will seem no fairer.

LADY'S MAN

A friend who's always been a lady's man
Sits sullenly on a bench in Washington Square
One Friday night, head cradled in his hands
Because some twenty-something called him "sir."
He's pushing fifty. Younger women who were
Taken for granted all his life have grown
Increasingly aloof, and haughtier.
He's graying—becoming bitter—and alone,
Actually doesn't think he should have known,
Always assumed that "time would pass him by."
(I, for my part, have never had anyone
But my late wife, long comatose when she died.)
Gaunt Gothic girls who throng the neon sidewalk
Ignore us both, engrossed in vulgar talk.

DECEPTIVE VIOLIN

Musée du Compagonnage, Tours, France

Stretched catgut strings undoubtedly are real;
Whorled tuning pegs, exquisite ebony:
But we've been duped by what we ought to see,
A close examination will reveal.
Such secrets does this artifact conceal!
No craftsman fashioned form from some rare tree,
No seasoned hardwoods curved compliantly,
No grain was sanded silken, fair to feel;
Leavings of genius scarcely understood
Enshrined among the wonders gathered here,
One would not choose to play it if one could,
As light might tease a delicate veneer—
For it's fine chocolate glazed like lacquered wood,
Chef-d'oeuvre of a great confectioner.

SPACE SHUTTLE *ENDEAVOUR*
CIRCLES WASHINGTON HIGH SCHOOL

San Francisco, September 21, 2012

The ragged quilt of autumn overcast
Suggests there may be nothing much to see.
Perhaps the shuttle has already passed,
Although we should have heard initially
The 747 that bears the load;
We would have heard the crowd outside as well;
Hundreds of adolescent cheers explode
As fierce anticipation starts to swell.
Then all at once, piercing a wall of cloud,
Two hundred feet beyond the classroom window,
The great plane slices past, immense and loud,
More striking from up here than from below.
Endeavour's a pilot fish fixed to a ray,
Whiteness astride white fuselage, white day.

LOVE SONG IN AN UNUSUAL KEY

The Flemish masters would have understood
My lifelong passion for the Rubensesque:
The female form when swollen to grotesque
Proportions stirs me as no frail waif could.
I love the bulging rolls and folds of flesh
That strain against the bright silk of a blouse,
A sexy waddle—when I'm feeling fresh—
Ignites a flame one thing alone will douse.
Plump peasant girls frolic beneath a sheen
Of fractured varnish, fiddler's tunes unheard;
High in the branches overhead, a bird
Exalts their rocking thighs. In such a scene
To praise the anorexic seems absurd!
(Some reading this will know just what I mean.)

FAT BLACK GIRL DRESSED IN GREEN

"For her own person,
It beggar'd all description..."
—William Shakespeare

Across the aisle—a crowded city bus—
She's unaware of ripening desire;
Beneath the straining vastness of her blouse
Soft folds of flesh enrapture and inspire.
Her dark eyes, almond-shaped, seem African,
Set in the mocha cushion of her face;
Full, pouting lips above a double chin
Urge us to kisses we will never taste.
When she leans forward, her unbridled breasts
Jiggle the winds of the imagination;
Swelling a thin skirt, massive buttocks press
Heavily on her seat, an invitation.
She seems at ease with such abundant beauty
While other girls chase slimness like a duty.

THE WINDMILL KIND

Interstate 580, Livermore, California

The gray-blond breathing hills of Altamont
Play host to legions even more quixotic
Than the gaunt horseman's giants. Who could want
A grander view than this one? So exotic!
The soft caress of wind—almost erotic—
Makes of propellers something sensual:
Metallic, fluid—not the least robotic—
They seem organic, ripe, botanical;
While muscled gusts, invisible, touch all,
Like time, a presence felt, if undefined.
A blown-glass autumn sky, a summer squall,
Spin on the bright blades of the windmill kind.
No quaint Dutch turrets these, with billowed sails,
But sentinels the anxious air assails.

A THOUSAND FLOWERS

i.m.: Mary Jean "MaJe" Kindschuh, died October 18, 2010

The day we met, chemo had made you bald,
Your voice a broken whisper. But I knew
No cancer could extinguish what shone through
In every glance and gesture. I recalled
Those gracious spirits I've known who seem called
To rectify the world, a golden few
Who touch our daily lives in all they do—
Whose goodness lingers, magnified tenfold
After their bodies enter memory.
A thousand flowers will bloom this coming spring,
A backyard garden you won't live to see—
More vivid for your loss—whose colors sing.
Such is your legacy, your victory:
Your love is undiminished by your passing.

THIS HOUSE YOU SHARED

i.m.: MaJe Kindschuh, 1958–2010

Three hundred square feet—like a small garage—
This house you shared throughout her final weeks,
Rebuilt to suit her cancer, plainly speaks
Of days each labored breath consumed an age.
Save for the love that lingers here, a cage
Is scarcely more confining; memory seeks
Oxygen tanks and walkers; longing leaks
Into each vacant corner, turns the page.
And yet her paintings, vibrant on these walls,
Proclaim a spirit never really gone;
A snow-white daffodil no doubt recalls
Spring's promise like a distant clarion;
Oblivious to grief's persistent squalls,
The potted amaryllis soldier on.

COTTAGES ONCE REMOTELY SITUATED

Row upon row of featureless tract housing,
All cinder block abused by bland earth tones,
Stare down a raw surf line's raucous carousing,
Dry grass and seawall where mean weather moans.
The sameness here and there is punctuated
By shingled shacks set well back from the street,
Cottages once remotely situated;
Sand dunes still sift beneath salt-soaked concrete
While trellised vines ascend some tiny yard—
Poor scrap emboldened by bright flowerbeds!
Here, the anemic earth is stunned and hard,
Leavings of last year's ivy brittle, dead.
And yet these quaint beach dwellings still retain
Grim dignity beneath late winter rain.

THE FAKE

Sunset District, San Francisco

One might imagine this whole neighborhood
Dissolves in August, just to reappear
A few weeks later, as smudged lines grow clear:
The counterfeit's imperfect, but quite good.
We'd sharpen these blurred edges, if we could;
Dew settles on the drenched gray grass like fear,
Lamp posts and hedges bleed, and grow severe;
Salt-sodden concrete seems misunderstood.
Our sense of unreality is subtle;
We're duped by such a clever forgery;
Such intricate details suggest rebuttal,
Like clumsy brushwork one must strain to see.
But when the skies clear in September, what will
Remain, and what seem foolish fantasy?

AT THE BOTANICAL GARDENS

Denver, Colorado

These gardens, late one winter afternoon,
Are silvered with a light that clings like frost;
The weather's crisp and cold. So much is lost
To time: an ancient willow—felled too soon—
Once ruled the Asian garden gone to ruin;
Gone, too, its dark reflection in the pool
Where twilight dusts the ice. Worn thin, grown cruel,
Wind in bare branches lisps a somber tune.
Somewhere a raven answers, bold and coarse;
Picking through shriveled grass, some smaller birds
Begin their awkward dance. Without remorse,
A sullen season stands its ground, and wards
Off green and pliant life, whose buried force
Dreams summer, a lush language beyond words.

EARTHQUAKE WEATHER

Dry leaves in San Francisco never turn
Those brilliant golds seen elsewhere by the Bay
Where foliage falls and festers, and they burn
To acrid smoke that brittle, heaped decay.
Indefinite skies seem neither blue nor gray
In numbed November, shivering between
Thin rain and sunlight, taunting the brief day;
Leaf-littered lawns lie nearer gray than green.
Each dawn's surprising warmth appears to mean
Late-sated summers sodden with sea salt;
Beneath our feet we navigate unseen
The fracture of the San Andreas Fault.
Time's an illusion here, the clock struck dumb;
One passing season mirrors those to come.

NATIONAL POETRY MONTH

In my in-box this morning, I discover
The "cruelest month" upon us once again:
Alfred A. Knopf comes wooing like a lover
Stirring desires undreamt of by spring rain.
A poem a day throughout the next four weeks,
From Keats to Leonard Cohen, Yeats to Rumi;
The verse-fed voice of commerce fairly shrieks;
Printed profusion threatens to undo me!
I rediscover Dryden, Amy Clampitt,
Arthur Rimbaud, Millay, and Wilfred Owen.
(I can't afford to buy them *all*, god damn it!
My cart on Amazon is overflowing!)
Greed, courtesy the siren call of Knopf,
Which—even if I could—I would not stopf.

THE DISUSED LINE

Grafton, Ohio

Sorrel and poke-weed smother broken ties,
The once-bright rails now oxidized to black;
Along the disused line bowed poles arise
Like vertebrae: some buried giant's back.
The wires are all down, or have gone slack
And dangle listless in the fetid air.
I've left for good; I won't be going back.
What reason is there to return to where
Summertime ran rough fingers through my hair?
The decades close behind me like a wound;
The eyes of relatives remaining there
Are like the eyes of people long since drowned.
Only the water tower names the place—
Blunt letters that the weather will erase.

AN EVENTUAL THAW

It's forty years at least since first I saw
Canadian glaciers crushed to sky-blue ice,
Great, patient peaks down which rocks sluice and slice
Beyond all hope of an eventual thaw.
Their heft has left the earth itself rubbed raw,
A bruised moraine no weather can entice,
The scarred site of an ancient sacrifice,
Where water fought the landscape to a draw.
These latter years, along the Palmer Range,
I've watched wind smoke the snow off jagged peaks—
A frozen conflagration, like some strange
White halo, when the mercury drops for weeks,
While winter waits—oblivious of change—
For the green, tender language summer speaks.

ON SPECIAL EDUCATION AND THE LAW

Of Special Education and the Law
I can report what I myself observed.
The similarities left me unnerved,
But I will vouch for everything I saw:
Even today, it still sticks in my craw.
I bore the accusations (undeserved),
The tantrums, senseless rage, and never swerved
From duty, though abuse had rubbed me raw.
In Special Ed, one learns to soldier on
When facing violence: hardened, as it were.
Kids who aren't cognizant of things they've done
Are called "disturbed." And yet I must aver
That in the law firms, dealing with someone
With these same qualities, one calls them "Sir."

AN OUNCE OF PREVENTION

"I would meet you upon this honestly."
—T. S. Eliot

We wish, of course, things had gone differently.
We know you had the very best intention,
But—may we please discuss this honestly?—
There was no "pound of cure," "ounce of prevention."
In retrospect, an early intervention
Might have prevented much that was to come;
One could say you were guilty by extension;
Still, you embraced the error—and then some!
The crippled heart too often is struck dumb
By lusts to which it hardly dare aspire:
A soft black thigh, dark breast, invites it home;
It tumbles helplessly from love's high wire.
Sex never was intended for *your* kind;
This too shall pass; just pay the pain no mind.

MY WASTREL WAYS

When I consider how my time is spent—
In sports bars where the television's loud,
Drinking to excess with a younger crowd—
I lack *cojones* even to repent
My wastrel ways. Being of artistic bent
Though only moderately well-endowed,
I'm lonely, slur my words, and—I'm not proud—
Embrace the cheap, more maudlin sentiment,
Hang out in seedy dives 'til much too late.
Plowed, hammered, smashed, intoxicated, pissed—
Blowing the foam off whole brigades of beers,
They also serve who only put on weight.
And Arthur Guinness, that great optimist,
Leased Saint James Brewery for nine hundred years!

FIVE SHOTS OF BUSHMILL'S

Columbus Avenue on Friday night
Is not, I'm told, what it was years ago;
The visual lisp of gaudy neon light
Paints broken pavements with a sickly glow
That once—in days of yore—may have been bright,
But speaks today of better times long gone.
Five shots of Bushmill's couldn't put things right;
I lost my right front tooth in The Saloon
When I slid from my bar stool to the floor,
Mouth bloodied, reputation in a ruin.
(Remind me not to pound them anymore;
Sometimes I can't imagine what I'm doing.)
Nowadays, I'm lost more often than I'm found;
But evening's young—let's have another round!

LAST WEDNESDAY NIGHT IN THE SALOON

This dive—established 1861—
The city's oldest, possibly its roughest,
Provides most North Beach poets with the grist
For several mills before an evening's done.
Consider Jimmy, graying and amiable,
A former hippie and a sometime biker,
Who loves my Stetson, likes to bend my ear:
How wistfully, how readily, he'll recall
The first time ever he killed a man. Thirteen,
Accosted in a restroom in the forties,
Before security cameras—thus unseen—
He brought the brutal stranger to his knees,
Pummeled him 'til (to use Jim's turn of phrase)
"He didn't work no more." The *first* time? Please!

MY DEATH GROWS MORE FAMILIAR AS I AGE

My death grows more familiar as I age:
Even this mild climate sharpens stars
But blurs the everyday with constant usage—
Too much complicity. Imagine Mars:
Remote, yet as insistent as old scars;
A faint pinprick of blood on the horizon,
Grim wanderer whose fate we know as ours,
Too distant—indistinct—to keep one's eyes on.
Death dogs me like this. With my life half gone
And each new day laid bare as a mistake,
The gentle promise of oblivion
Seems all the comfort I can hope to take.
The pulse that slows with age will one day still;
I bear its burdens now by force of will.

SLIGHT ABERRATIONS

A chest X-ray: faint shadow on one lung
(Of course it couldn't possibly be serious,
Anxious, unnerved, and still morbidly curious—
Practically certain nothing's really wrong,
Just some congestion, knew it all along,
Slight aberrations really shouldn't worry us.)
Most of our demons turn out to be spurious,
Figments of our unfettered fears grown strong.
But how dare we to suppose we may be mortal,
We, who once held Forever in our hands?
We're loath to take our place at that dark portal
Whose chilling threshold's thrall no one withstands.
Whatever then awaits makes of us all
Unspeakable, unyielding demands.

FOR ONE SURREAL MOMENT

My right front tooth was shattered in a bar
When I slipped from a stool and hit the floor.
I won't be swigging Bushmill's anymore;
I guess I pushed the envelope too far.
The temporary crown just felt bizarre,
Strange underneath my tongue, hard to ignore:
Along the gum line everything was sore,
Inflamed and bleeding, nothing up to par.
Why am I even bothering to explain?
For one surreal moment, around the chair,
In broken English—heedless of my pain—
A dozen Russian ladies with bright hair
Gruffly debated shades of porcelain.
I wouldn't have been anywhere but there.

DO-IT-YOURSELF CREMATORIUM

Depicted on the cardboard box, it seems
Like a chrome thermos, a martini shaker—
Neither the stuff of nightmares nor of dreams—
A grisly bauble waiting for a taker.
This is the relic that will make or break her,
Our pallid, flaxen-headed, bright sprite Death,
Receiving, should the grave itself forsake her,
As smoke and ash the chill of her stilled breath.
And there it sits, conspicuous beneath
Cartons of four-way plugs, bright bins of nails;
This tasteless thing inviting disbelief:
The crassness of the marketplace prevails.
It's probably illegal anyway;
Who could—who would—be bold enough to say?

A SEASON OF REPOSE

At issue before the Board of Education
Is who in fact resides in San Francisco,
Neither a quick nor firm determination:
Sometimes it's really difficult to know.
The guidelines are bizarre and somewhat Zen:
Home is "a season of repose," "sweet rest,"
"A permanence," "a solace now and then,"
"That haven one evokes." The die is cast:
The line to reach the podium is long;
Speakers loom large on liquid crystal screens,
The gallery, grown several hundred strong,
Argue among themselves what all this means.
Home, once the refuge of a restless heart,
May be a cell phone number, shopping cart.

GROUNDHOG DAY

A pleasant little critter all in all,
Though nature rarely panders to the cute:
One moment in weak light, and it will scoot
Back down the burrow. Whether shadows crawl,
Or don't, can't matter to a thing so small;
In this hygienic age the point is moot;
We track storm clouds by satellite and shoot
Dry ice at summer knowing rain will fall.
Perhaps the old traditions keep us prudent,
Refashioning our kinship with the Earth;
Reminding us each leaf was once a portent.
Or are these children's stories, of no worth
Save that they cause our hearts to reinvent
A time whose simple charms still call us forth?

CAPTAIN AHAB RUNNING FOR A BUS

"... from hell's heart I stab at thee; for hate's sake I spit my last breath at thee."
—Moby-Dick, Chapter 135

Though land-bound, it's still very large, and white,
And—in its way—ferocious as the Whale.
Since buses run infrequently at night,
Our amputee's determined to prevail
Against this diesel demon pulling out,
Whose grunting, smoky bulk he staggers toward.
The baleen-headed cane he waves about
Conceals a full harpoon, not just a sword,
But this proves useless, as the heaving beast,
All steel and rivets, will not be detained;
The Captain's ire is palpably increased
And, like a tempest, rages unrestrained.
Unmanned, he curses this strange century
More treacherous than any savage sea.

THE DARKNESS COILED IN COMMON THINGS

> *"He reported that ghosts thronged about him as he climbed the stairs*
> *to bed, trying to push him back down. At the top of the stairs, he*
> *was sometimes met by a green woman with tusks."*
> —Jonathan Rosen, *"Doubles: Wilkie Collins's Shadow*
> *Selves," in the "New Yorker"*

Forget the green-faced woman with the fangs,
The midnight ghosts that force you down the stairs,
The scheming wraiths that take you unawares,
The slender thread by which your sane life hangs.
Forget the darkness coiled in common things—
A pair of scissors, empty sherry glass—
Lace curtains know the worst will come to pass.
Bless laudanum, the scant relief it brings.
The rotten moon is risen like a diamond,
Or like the crazed gaze of a woman in white:
Don't fear the dark, but dread what lies beyond,
The anguished stars like shattered bits of light.
Illness will have you—you are moribund—
But you transcend it, every word you write.

AN ELEGY AND A BIRTHDAY CARD, FOR MAY 17, 2011

i.m.: Adrienne Stengel, 1957–2006

Pious disciple of Bahá'u'lláh,
You knew this life was not the only one:
A dizzy dance with death, a brief hurrah.
Five years have passed away since you've been gone.
Your birthday's here, sees summer coming on,
Wind silvering through eucalyptus leaves,
Sweet sadness spreading like soft solstice sun.
While we weren't lovers, part of me still grieves.
Perhaps that person's happiest who believes,
Not just in God's grace, but in our world's, too,
Who lives a glory no one else perceives,
A casual greatness granted to too few.
You left stepchildren and a husband; they
Can scarcely miss you as I do today.

DENVER LIGHT

Twilight in Denver's a metallic light,
Like beaten gold against cold winter sky—
A ledger where denuded branches write
Demotic ciphers for the anxious eye.
A hawk's an errant comma that may fly
By chance across this bleak illumination;
Nature, of course, has dotted every "i,"
But what explains such random punctuation?
These gilded clouds eschew all explanation;
They seem a momentary glimpse of Heaven;
Religions of deceit and obfuscation
Deny so pure a grace so freely given.
Then gold is tarnished into *verdigris*—
Hinting at darker palettes yet to be.

EXCEPT FOR SUMMER

As decades fall away like peel from fruit,
I've grown unsure of nearly everything—
The past, as much as what the years may bring—
Grown heavier, more wrinkled, bald to boot.
Except for summer, I wouldn't give a hoot
For my decline, my life's unraveling,
Resigned to some eventual reckoning,
My days familiar as a well-worn suit.
But these September evenings—still so warm,
When crickets' ruckus swells the early dark—
These are the nights I fear I'll come to harm:
When every firefly's a precious spark,
My brittle longings fusing with the swarm
Like nervous travelers waiting to embark.

HARD WATER

Two iron spigots—one for hot, one cold—
Disgorged their burden in a porcelain sink:
Water so crisp and clear that every drink
Surprised us, fecund topsoil making bold
Assertions on the valley of the tongue.
Herein were mingled summer pastures strewn
With amputated flowers; autumn's ruin;
The hardened nuggets of last season's dung.
From deeper underground a taste arose
Of tungsten, copper, manganese, and tin:
A faint metallic bitterness disclosed
Little by little, like juniper from gin—
Deepest of all, the stagnant blood of those
The hungry hoarder earth had gathered in.

HOUSES SWEPT SEAWARD, BURNING

Japanese earthquake and tsunami, March 11, 2011

Live footage streaming from the foreign news
Shows devastation not to be believed:
Houses swept seaward, burning. We're relieved
To have been spared this; panoramic views
Of skyscrapers encased in mud confuse
And frighten. We have somehow been deceived
Concerning nature's goodness, and we're grieved;
There's no relief, whatever words we choose.
In San Francisco, public school students
Are kept at home. Authorities seem unclear
About the awful weight of these events:
Tsunamis in Japan will not reach here,
Too far away to be of consequence;
One more catastrophe to fuel our fear.

GREGORY PECK AND AVA GARDNER

Japanese earthquake and tsunami, March 11, 2011

The fallout from Japan has spread this far,
And stirring in my memory tonight,
Grim Gregory Peck and drunken Ava Gardner
Trade barbs in finely nuanced black and white.
Spring rain has cleansed the air, yet this soft light
Has something strange about it, like a fire—
Not quite an omen—ready to ignite:
Some dark fear or a long-repressed desire.
The tally of the drowned climbs ever higher
Thousands of miles across the torn gray seas;
In San Francisco, a more subtle choir
Laments our loss: thin, wind-beleaguered trees.
We are not gathered just yet on the beach;
But even here we feel Doomsday's cold reach.

THE LAKE REMEMBERED
FROM YOUR CHILDHOOD

The lake remembered from your childhood
We couldn't find—it must have been nearby.
A frozen local pond was near as good:
A fallen fragment of the winter sky
Nestled in brown and brittle prairie grass.
Just north of Colorado Springs, we stopped
At a little ice cream shop we chanced to pass,
Still open in December. Mercury dropped
As the light faltered, while we sat inside
Watching a tiny Christmas train go round
And round. We talked of loved ones who had died—
My wife, your partner—longings lost and found.
Somewhere, still unseen waters seemed to hold
Dark promises—oblivion, sweet and cold.

EARTH'S ABUNDANT BEAUTY

An actual sunset haunted Munch's "The Scream,"
Historians believe: The Krakatau
Explosion, 1883, would seem
Responsible for bloodied skies. Allow
For superstition, and the sects that now
Predict the imminence of Judgment Day
Become more understandable. Somehow
Fierce luminosity frightens us away
From earth's abundant beauty. Who can say
Just what the problem is with the transcendent?
Cloud banks ablaze with dubious portents may
Be terrifying just because resplendent.
The end is near, as it has always been:
Heaven is *here*, and welcomes us all in.

OUR FAITH IN WORDS

"Joy can't be faked. Joy is just there."
—*From "Black Lab," 2006*

Reading the latest poems by David Young,
I think again of brown September fields
Outside of Oberlin, when summer yields
Slowly to autumn, but the light is strong.
I guess I knew the answer all along:
How Nature's casual optimism shields
The heart from sorrow, how the world wields
A bullfrog's baritone, a warbler's song.
David, you're well past seventy by now,
As I'm past fifty. We have both lost wives.
Our faith in words still cultivates somehow
A verdant garden where renewal thrives
Even in grief, determined to endow
What's purest in us—deepest—what survives.

EUCALYPTUS IN A HEAT WAVE

Heat climbs in ragged ribbons from the pavement,
The Avenues unseasonably hot,
Thick coastal fogs all vanished. We are not
Accustomed to such weather; summer's spent
Shivering in mist, its natural element:
Seasons are something the Good Lord forgot
When He made San Francisco. Like dry rot,
May settles in; its energies relent.
When I arrived, now twenty-odd years ago,
I found the climate redolent of ghosts;
The sodden eucalyptus groves that grow
Where ancient redwoods fell impressed me most.
In this unusual warmth the limp leaves glow
Like fading memories, already lost.

WHY EVERY DAY
IS HARDER THAN THE LAST

Insipid weather; nothing new of note:
This coastal city mimics brooding skies;
A blunt gray sadness lingering in the eyes
Of passing strangers has us by the throat.
Such are the tired lives we've learned by rote,
Whose disappointments we cannot disguise:
The dull routine we cling to sometimes buys
A moment's solace, but the point is moot.
Why every day is harder than the last
No one can say for sure, though none deny it;
Our grief is unexceptional, if vast,
Too subtle to acknowledge or decry it.
Halfheartedly, the damaged die is cast;
This is our mettle; these, the times that try it.

WHAT HOLDS US HERE

The sonnets of the thirteenth century
Idealized love in ways beyond us now.
These frenzied lives we lead will not allow
Our contemplating anything too deeply.
Petrarch's beloved Laura might prove to be
Pitted with plague scars, or an ill-bred sow;
Could we but see her, we would disavow
Her image seared upon eternity.
Love's undiminished by such imperfection:
Eyes rimmed with wrinkles are where sadness shines,
Hair thinned to brightness startles by its beauty.
Our aging bodies will not pass inspection,
Grown brittle as Victorian Valentines;
And yet what holds us here is more than duty.

WINDOWS ON IRVING STREET

Rain in late May accosts the Avenues.
Fog blankets the drenched dimness like regret:
Worn-weary pavements wear a sheen of wet;
Potholes recall the soles of ragged shoes.
If sun breaks through these sullen clouds, it's news;
It's called the Sunset District—true—and yet
After a year, I've hardly seen a sunset,
Just overcast imbued with hopeful hues.
On Irving Street, the Chinese bakeries
Sell red bean dumplings late into the night,
Hawk fortune cookies' banal prophecies,
Their rain-ripe windows poultices of light
Throbbing against the hour's uncertainties,
Slithering scripts the wind has yet to write.

OUR ORPHANED ENGLISH HAS NO NAMES

Long summer evenings, in the failing light,
On quiet sidewalks in the Sunset District,
Elderly men at tables shuffle bright
Square tiles across a playing board. We're tricked
By curiosity and watch their games
If we are passing by, guessing at rules:
For this, our orphaned English has no names;
Carved pieces stud the humid dark like jewels.
Pale Chinese ghosts, translucent memories.
Emblazoned characters, bright red or blue,
Grasped in thin, fluttering hands, trace histories
Of what a language dare—and dare not—do.
These words we cannot read are couched in silence;
A text from ages past, or ages hence.

THE SUTRO SCHOONER

The crown of Sutro Tower, in wet weather,
Seems a three-masted schooner sailing waves
Of churning fog. Summer's cold heart behaves
Badly; these early mornings rush together
Like a white surf line straining at its tether,
The ghost of some tsunami that still craves
Our sunken land, our drowned in brine-drenched graves—
Frenzied and foul, yet lighter than a feather.
The Sutro Schooner floats on salty carnage
Such as the sleeping city dare not dream:
Flotsam from which there's nothing much to salvage,
The shifting shoreline like a ruptured seam.
Some nights the calm Pacific's whims turn savage,
Rank reefs of water stifling a scream.

SELF-PORTRAIT IN A BATHROOM MIRROR

My morning shower spits needles of wet heat,
Scorching my back like some grim martyrdom;
The beard I coarsely trim is flecked with white,
A woeful harbinger of things to come.
This misted glass before me—cheaply backed
With tarnished silver peppered through with rust—
Reflects a weary icon with a crack,
Set in base metal, all grave rapture lost.
But mine is not the pious martyr's sigh
Whose soul ascends a brilliant plume of breath;
Flesh that now loosely sags below each eye
Speaks of dust-dreaming bones that lie beneath:
My eyes, gray-blue as late November sky,
Like coins pressed presciently against my death.

THE MAN WHOSE LIFE I MIGHT HAVE LED

I almost glimpse the contours of his face
Some mornings in the bathroom mirror, aware
The sorrow in his eyes is always there,
A consequence of each new day's disgrace.
The differences are difficult to place
But undeniable—his dark, thick hair,
Expensive suits that I would never wear,
A sense of style, an enviable grace.
At 54, my dreams elude me still;
What little I've learned of living's linked to loss.
The man whose life I might have led must fill
These worn-out shoes, these hours, this dreary dross.
One need not be a murderer to kill,
In painful increments, what never was.

GLASS AND CÉZANNE

It hovers on the threshold of abstraction,
Cézanne's late rendering of Mont Sainte-Victoire:
These clustered brushstrokes in which fields are
As firm and solid as the day's perfection,
Where stony clouds create a misdirection,
Confusing peak and sky. To come so far,
And yet retain in every vivid bar
Of color something of the land's attraction!
In Philip Glass's brisk arpeggios
We find a sonic likeness of the scene:
A music sharply chiseled that still flows
Into a stillness usually unseen
'Til every note and semi-quaver glows
Like the determined mountain of Cézanne.

ONE FLICKERING STREETLIGHT

One flickering streetlight stutters light and shadow,
A feeble radiance no eye relies on;
Morning arrives disconsolately sad, though
Pale gray yawns absently on the horizon;
Cumulus writhe across uneasy skies. On
The opposite curb, three squat recycling bins
Fester in silence. Night has no disguise on;
The day's already old as it begins.
Daylight discloses multitudes of sins;
The world's essential mediocrity
Stands wholly naked. Anyone would wince
At such a blemished scene—but who's to see?
One flickering streetlight on a disused street
Alone observes the wounded dark's retreat.

THE LIE

In places where the clouds had worn away,
We glimpsed the emptiness that lay beyond:
A sort of dullness, featureless and gray,
Polluted water in a stagnant pond.
Concerning God—to our dismay—we found
Thousands came forth who claimed to be the One;
Each drunken would-be Christ displayed a wound
Some doubting Thomas would then dote upon.
Churches were empty, congregations gone;
In mosques and temples, a great rummage sale
Commenced as sacred trappings were torn down;
Communion wine was quaffed like roadhouse ale.
Some thought it best that we'd outlived the lie;
Some trembled at the vast, unfeeling sky.

WHEN WE IMAGINE ANGELS

When we imagine angels, we see wings,
But we have no desire now for flight;
The losses life inexorably brings
Seem not to stem from unseen realms of light.
The well-toned seraphim who so delight
Painters and sculptors are mere artifice;
An ancient elm tree shouldering the blight
Possesses more grim dignity than this.
We tap dance on the edge of the abyss
While strolling calmly down a shaded street;
Wind moans across a wounded precipice
There on the asphalt underneath our feet.
As for the seraphim, by now we know—
What wings we had were shredded long ago.

A FRIEND WHO IS CRITICALLY ILL

Ironically, it was Bob Dylan's birthday
The day I opened Wendy's grim email
Detailing how your lungs had begun to fail
And you were growing weaker by the day.
Jaimes, there's so very much I'd like to say:
I miss the drunken evenings when we'd rail
Against the state of poetry, dark ale,
Those Sixties chestnuts we both loved to play.
"Lily, Rosemary, and the Jack of Hearts,"
Bob's convoluted Western mystery—
Truth and illusion playing so many parts—
Has lost what power it had to comfort me.
You'd solved the riddle, wanted me to see;
Now, grief steals in each time the music starts.

YOU GREW A GOATEE

You grew a goatee in those final weeks:
Its hopeful gray adorned your speechless lips.
(After a tracheotomy, who speaks?)
Low, labored breathing, harsh electric blips
From the surrounding monitors were all
The sounds remained as silences unfurled;
No blather breached that bubble shrunk so small
Your sickbed seemed to dwarf the wider world.
You must have sensed that you had only days,
And yet you sprouted this thin, tentative thing—
A last defiant act because it says
You meant to make some changes, notwithstanding.
Your wasted body was already finished,
But death found you well-groomed, pride undiminished.

IN MEMORY OF JAIMES ALSOP, 1943-2011

Editor and friend, died June 23, 2011

That final evening at the hospital,
Bright painted Buddha serene upon your nightstand,
A bowl of golden sunflowers placed by hand,
The struggle of your breath grown faint and small:
These are among the details I'll recall.
Your name contained your illness, Mr. ALSop—
Slow foxfire in the nerves that would not stop,
Stick-figure limbs, bent body's scribbled scrawl;
In these last weeks, your weakness was a cage.
Your eyes, quite lively in a ruined face,
Still welcomed visitors, sought to encourage,
Rekindled friendships nothing could replace.
Your patient wisdom, silent tutelage,
Gave vivid voice to my *Disfigured Grace.*

BIRD AND COWS

Inspired by the Ken Burns film "Jazz."

Someone has told him, half in jest, that cows
Are very fond of music. Now the "Bird,"
Car idling in a midnight pasture, blows
Cool alto sax for an astonished herd.
Bewildered livestock turn their gaze horn-ward,
The jazz man's leaning figure doubled in
The turgid depths of bovine eyes, each chord
A galaxy poised waiting to begin.
The horn's unfurling cry is almost human,
Decries the agony of what it means
To be a cow—and what to be a man—
What grand improvisations lie between.
The onyx sky transcribes ascending bars
Brilliant with crisp arpeggios of stars.

ORDINARY QUARTERS

23 Fitzroy Road, London

Sylvia Plath and William Butler Yeats
Shared the same London flat some years apart—
A small, ill-lighted place, one speculates—
Poor refuge for a vulnerable heart.
In a shop window, Yeats beheld a ball
Dancing aloft on silver jets of spray,
Pictured a laughing Irish waterfall,
Imagined "The Lake Isle of Innisfree."
Plath, separated, two young kids in tow,
Labored long nights to crystallize her pain:
Lines spun so fine whole phrases seemed to glow,
Fat for the fire in an anguished brain.
Ordinary quarters, average neighborhood—
I would arise and go there, if I could.

PICKLE MEDITATIONS

Let's have a sonnet with a pickle in it—
Plump, unbound mummy from a distant age,
Adrift in brine—a warty Buddha sage
That, by its changelessness, will no doubt fit
In dill's arcane tradition. Were it lit,
We might mistake it for a green cigar
Spewing its smoke in some expatriate bar,
Tobacco tinged with garlic and dry wit.
Bite into pickles just to hear the crunch,
A crisp percussion for a piccolo;
A summit meeting or a casual lunch
Feels the more festive for its verdant glow;
The taste seems to impart—it's just a hunch—
That simple, salty wisdom pickles know.

NO TENDER RADIANCE FILLS MY WORLD

Most of my life—until just years ago—
Every few months had a specific *feeling*,
Each so distinctive that I came to know
The texture of it, found its touch revealing.
These days, no tender radiance fills my world
I might one day recall or recognize;
No further revelations are unfurled;
There is a sort of deadness in my eyes.
I've no idea whether other people
Experience deep loss in quite this way;
What light informs my path is thin and feeble;
Once-vivid colors bleed to dirty gray.
Yet I remember still when each new dawn
Ignited ecstasies now decades gone.

TODAY I FEEL AS BURDENED
AS THE WEATHER

Today I feel as burdened as the weather:
A thin, embittered pallor claims the Bay;
Cumulus strain uneasily at their tether;
Across dull water, headlands fade and fray.
This is a *resolutely* average day,
Bereft of any noble expectations;
A fetid coastal fog evokes decay,
Lost aspirations, keenly felt frustrations.
An atmosphere of quiet resignation
Arises from the paucity of words,
The fact there really isn't an occasion
To point a maimed, accusing finger towards.
Nothing is wrong, but clearly, nothing's right:
A sullenness, a nasty trick of light.

A LITTLE WATER MUSIC

Fog dims our frigid coast to monochrome
This bitter winter: moisture borne on air.
Water—that rogue—can easily become
Slyly insinuated everywhere;
Even in barren lands, it may ensnare
Burnt dust too airily dull to harbor life;
As ice in passing comets, it may tear
A scar across night skies. Impudent knife,
It cleaves through mighty mountains; it is wife
To salt—a long entanglement of tears—
A romance fraught with bitterness and strife.
And then there are the burdens water bears—
Green, brine-encrusted murmurs of drowned gods,
Seas parted by a hundred Moses' rods.

THE EXPURGATED VERSION

What strange chain of events compelled me here?
Ordinary moments redolent of pain,
Private regrets impossible to explain,
Settle like dusty neon on my beer.
For part of every day I disappear—
Or wish I could. Such pleasures as remain
Ring true, but seem diluted: John Coltrane
Burnishes afternoon's decayed veneer.
A month from now, I will turn 54.
I want a woman I won't ever have.
My failures throng around me, keeping score.
Aches in my teeth confirm I'm still alive.
Yet summer slyly hints at something more,
Some revelation shortly to arrive.

MY TENURE ON THIS EARTH

Tired today, I fell on Park Presidio,
The pale, cracked asphalt in the early light
A pitted wasteland, pitiless and white;
Oncoming traffic didn't even slow.
I should have been run over years ago:
Across the decades I have never quite
Suppressed the panic urging me to flight,
Established balance, known which way to go.
Shadowy terrors pool and collect
In morning's corners as I struggle forth.
Too much I love has fallen to neglect;
I can't tell, now, what anything is worth.
Already I'm beginning to suspect
I've overstayed my tenure on this earth.

LASCAUX

The paintings in the caverns at Lascaux
Display an elegance born of desperation.
That life was hard twelve thousand years ago
No one disputes. What wounded jubilation,
What courage in a hopeless situation,
Infused with grace and beauty a dark rite
Meant to bring meat in times of near starvation,
Subdue great beasts as panicked herds took flight?
They limned their prey on stone by firelight
Using the charred debris of shattered spears:
The pictures' simple power, awed delight,
Still resonate across long, lonely years.
Here are the seeds. Picasso and Gauguin
Owe much to nameless paleolithic man.

THESE SOILED ANGELS

A dapper, elderly Latino man,
Whom I see at the bus stop every morning
Headed for Mass, is certain that he can
Find in black pigeons foraging a warning.
The filthy birds, he says, are fallen doves
With only littered streets to make a home in;
Descended from the silver birds God loves,
These soiled angels are an evil omen.
As harbingers of squalor and disease,
The city's long sought to eradicate them—
Arnoldo prophesies catastrophes
Should we poor sinners fail to venerate them:
The world will end when the last pigeon dies,
God's vengeance raining blood from boiling skies.

MY PRODUCTIVE COUGH

Two days of illness. My productive cough
Wrote seven plays, five novels, ninety poems;
To top it off (as if that weren't enough),
Composed a choral setting for the *Psalms*.
The *Mucus Manifesto*, blithely penned
By that same phlegm I thoughtlessly expelled,
Proclaimed the "tracheal bondage" at an end,
Oppression by the lungs soon to be quelled.
And all the while, I lingered in a daze,
As that green, viscous goo displayed sheer brilliance,
An infinite capacity to amaze;
My own work seemed of little consequence.
Annoyed by its propensity to vex,
I wiped the bugger out with one Kleenex.

OUR MAD CLIMATE

After reading the sonnets of Edna St. Vincent Millay

Warm sun blows green and golden through a day
No better—and no worse—than any other;
Just hours ago these curdled skies were gray,
Chastened beneath the burden of hard weather.
At times, I really start to wonder whether
This world isn't some elaborate joke.
What signs we have, if taken all together,
Suggest our lives are little more than smoke.
Cynic within, perhaps its time you spoke:
Exotic plants embolden Golden Gate Park;
Transplanted trees—uncertain—go for broke,
Caught in a struggle to forestall the dark,
But nothing takes root in this forsaken soil
That our mad climate soon enough won't spoil.

THE ENGLISH AUTHOR
BRAVED NIAGARA FALLS

*"It would be hard for a man to stand nearer God
than he does there."*
　　　—Charles Dickens in a letter to John Forster, 1842

The English author braved Niagara Falls,
Forgave the foibles of our unformed nation:
Tobacco spittle, sodden lodging walls,
Accents too crude for proper conversation.
White, warring waters wholly swept away
The cities' stench, the scourge of slavery,
Festering marshes fetid with decay
Where iridescent flies droned damningly.
No gentle zephyr in bright Kentish fields
Raged with such raw—such elemental—force;
Secrets the teeming ages had concealed
Spewed from the coiling chaos at the source:
Creation's heart, laid bare for all to see,
Stripped of false pretense and gentility.

REMEMBERING SAMUEL

"The shrine whose shape I am
Has a fringe of fire."
　　　　　—Samuel Menashe, 1925–2011

I met you once in a West Village bar
Where you were featured in the early Eighties,
Had no idea then how wise you were,
But blessed the gift of poems as fine as these.
Concision culled from daily verities,
Brief verses, splendid gems, enriched each page:
You caught the word's capacity to please,
Attuned to every nuance of our age.
Already—not yet sixty—a graying sage,
You would not autograph a book to "Bob,"
But with a gentle firmness voiced outrage
At commonplace diminutives that rob
Scriptural grandeur from our given names,
Your silver hair like softly chiding flames.

AN ABANDONED SANATORIUM
IN COLORADO

Consumption, in the nineteenth century,
Was a death sentence unimagined now.
Keats—trained in healing—bled internally,
And knew how little time fate would allow.
A dribbled darkness on a linen pillow
Spilled from one ear, and spelled impending doom;
His breath grew labored and his prospects shallow,
The vaulted sky itself a stifling tomb.
Some hoped for miracles in mountain air;
Others sought solace in a kinder climate;
All lingered on the margins of despair:
Theirs, dwindling days by any estimate.
Nowadays, a squalid light has overtaken
The vacant sickrooms of the once forsaken.

A WOUNDED MOON
ENSNARED BY HIGHWAY WIRES

Lake Texoma, near Norman, Oklahoma

The deadly "fiddle back" brown recluse spider;
A wounded moon ensnared by highway wires;
A dull brown lake as cloudy as new cider;
A thin horizon smudged by derrick fires;
The sultry Texas-Oklahoma border;
A field station where my dad was teaching;
Long, moth-thronged dusks above a morbid water;
A lunar plain that scarcely seemed worth reaching.
Such was midsummer 1969;
I'd just turned twelve, sex was a mystery,
America's dream already in decline,
Conflicts in Asia raging pointlessly.
I saw myself in that entangled moon,
Poised to escape an age that ends too soon.

YELLOW STUCCO

The house on Elm, where my grandparents lived,
A tree with sour green apples in the back,
Wore yellow stucco siding, which I loved;
Smog blown from Cleveland leavened it with black.
These days, it seems, there isn't any lack
Of recollections from those distant years:
The mill downtown, the disused railroad track,
Midsummer lilacs take me unawares.
However grim my adult life appears—
However grim my childhood, in its way—
The roughness of old stucco still repairs
Much of the aging world's perceived decay.
My fingertips retain the memory
Of textured walls, their strange topography.

HIS ACCENT MAKES US
WANT TO HEAR HIM TALK

Belgrade, via Chicago and New York:
Part streetwise kid, part European sage,
His accent makes us want to hear him talk,
Much though his poems enrich the printed page.
Serbian surname anglicized to Simic,
He's ditched the Slavic moniker of youth;
A taut surrealism many mimic
Finds in the plainest things a darker truth.
Greeting the Master Class at our first session
With anecdotes that challenge and beguile
(Thirty years on, I blush at this confession),
He uses words that often make me smile,
Which no transcription really quite describes:
"I got—whaddya call 'em—yeah, good *wibes*."

LOGGING ON

Apparently Cyndi Lauper's had a face lift,
And Lindsay Lohan's broken her parole,
Unsightly warts are easy to control,
Conspicuous consumption's the new thrift.
Don't let us give astrology short shrift:
Bright constellations prance about the pole,
Assure us our vague lives may yet be whole,
The future can be *read*—you catch the drift?
Meanwhile, deep in our collective brain,
Lurk rumors of another, darker, sort:
Atomic clouds too toxic to contain,
Orphans of bloated belly, feeble heart,
Starving in places parched for want of rain,
Whose agony there's no need to report.

JET TRAILS BISECTED IN A SUNSET SKY

The days ahead affront us, raw and lean
As ghetto trees, leaving the worst unsaid;
Each loss—one out of many—seems to mean
Less left to cherish, more perhaps to dread.
Would that the future offered us instead
Jet trails bisected in a sunset sky,
A glowing cross laid on a field of red,
Seeming to deepen as spent shadows die.
This is no age for omens. Burning high
Above gaunt shipyard derricks streaked with rust,
It lingers for a moment in the eye:
A crucifix of frozen mist and dust.
No symbol, it portends no higher duty,
Yet heals the world a little by its beauty.

SET IN STONE

The malaise grows more trenchant every year.
Though we've perhaps been fortunate in life,
We sense there's little under the veneer
Except a chill that hones us like a knife.
Few reassurances are set in stone:
A pigeon's tracks preserved in brown concrete
Where an unnoticed bird, now decades gone,
Traced constellations with its star-shaped feet;
A painted boulder lovingly inscribed
Gracing a manicured suburban lawn
That welcomes an addition to the tribe,
Names and proclaims a baby yet unborn.
Such unpretentious diamonds in the rough!
If they are all we have, they are enough.

THE LIGHT THAT POOLS
UPON A WOMAN'S THIGH

Like ice in frozen climates, grief expands
Until it wears away our firm resolve.
It is a calm catastrophe—like love,
Like time that hangs too heavy on our hands.
Our dreams exact ridiculous demands
As we grow older: so much still to prove,
Unfriendly weather marshaling above,
No remnants left of our once-splendid plans.
The light that pools upon a woman's thigh
Recedes into oblivion like a dream,
A rumor in a corner of one eye;
Only anxieties are what they seem.
Even when young we struggled not to cry,
Who now wake daily stifling a scream.

THE WEIGHT OF ENDED THINGS

My first brief kiss occurred at forty-one,
Sex not long afterwards. While worth the wait,
Love—when at last it blossomed—came too late
To heal the harm the lonely years had done;
By early middle age, the fight had gone
Clean out of me. I still anticipate
New disappointments, carrying the weight
Of ended things before they have begun.
You wear your beauty tenderly, and yet
I know the hesitation in your eyes—
Fathomless gemstones burning soft and wet,
Holding blunt truths *in lieu* of kinder lies,
Looting the gutted cities of regret
From whose stunned dust no phoenix dare arise.

THE PERFORMANCE

I would be thought a failure by any standard;
By now I know it probably is true.
I'm poorly recompensed for what I do;
My life, in its banality, is hard.
Moist summer sunlight claws across the yard,
Stretches its warm and dusty fingers through
The neighbor's fence—does what it has to do—
A stage magician proffering a card.
This deck's been marked by charlatans galore;
The worn days scatter like a clumsy hand,
Spelling regrets I scarcely understand,
Arranged in strange suits never seen before.
Somehow, things haven't turned out as I planned.
I should have left the audience wanting more.

INDEX OF TITLES

ABOUT THE AUTHOR

BORN IN MICHIGAN IN 1957 and raised in northern New Jersey, Robert Lavett Smith now lives in San Francisco, where for the past fourteen years he has worked as a Special Education Paraprofessional at George Washington High School in the Richmond District, assisting students with a range of disabilities. He holds a B.A in French from Oberlin College, where he also studied creative writing with Stuart Friebert and David Young. Subsequently, he earned an M.A. in English with an emphasis in writing from the University of New Hampshire, studying with Charles Simic and Mekeel McBride. In 1982, after graduating from UNH, he was a member of the Master Class at the 92nd Street Y in New York City, where he studied with Galway Kinnell.

In addition to *Smoke In Cold Weather*, he has authored four small-press chapbooks and one previous full-length effort, *Everything Moves With A Disfigured Grace* (Alsop Review Press, 2006). All of these are free verse works. This new collection is his first foray into formalism.

A NOTE ON THE FONTS

This book is set in High Tower Text, designed by American type designer Tobias Frere-Jones in 1996 and based on Nicolas Jensen's 1470 Venetian roman. Titles are set in Gotham Black, one of a family of geometric sans-serif digital typefaces modeled on New York City street signs and designed by Frere-Jones in 2000.

CPSIA information can be obtained
at www.ICGtesting.com
Printed in the USA
BVHW030804280119
538836BV00001B/14/P